# The Phoenician Sonnets

Mediterranean mysteries along
ancient trading routes

Stephen Stockwell

Talle
budgerra
Press

**The Phoenician Sonnets**
Mediterranean mysteries along ancient trading routes

First published in Australia by Tallebudgera Press 2023
ABN 62 213 504 925
tallebudgerapress@gmail.com

Copyright © Stephen Stockwell 2023
All Rights Reserved

 A catalogue record for this book is available from the National Library of Australia

ISBN: 978-0-6451848-2-2 (pbk)
ISBN: 978-0-6451848-3-9 (ebk)

Written and illustrated by Stephen Stockwell © 2023
Front cover image by: Tarskaya_Tatiana © Shutterstock
Back cover, author photo by Blasius Erlinger ©

Typesetting and design by Publicious Book Publishing
Published in collaboration with Publicious Book Publishing
www.publicious.com.au

No part of this book may be reproduced in any form, by photocopying or by any electronic or mechanical means, including information storage or retrieval systems, without permission in writing from both the copyright owner and the publisher of this book.

For Hugo and Hallie, adventurers.

# Contents

| | |
|---|---|
| Preface | i |
| Notes on Terminology | v |
| Chronology | vi |
| | |
| Introduction | 1 |
| | |
| Homeland | 15 |
| Ugarit – Arwad – Byblos – Beirut – Sidon – Sarepta – Tyre – Dor – South | |
| | |
| Greek Sphere of Influence | 49 |
| Kition – Rhodes – Ionian Coast – Aegean – Athens – Crete – Peloponnese – Sicily | |
| | |
| Carthage and West | 83 |
| Carthage – Sardinia – Tyrrhenian Sea – Heracles' Pillars – Cadiz – Morocco | |
| | |
| Conclusion | 109 |
| | |
| Essay: The History of Phoenician-Greek Interaction | 118 |
| Museums and Selected Sites Visited | 137 |
| Top Ten Phoenician Books | 141 |

# Preface

"What is it with you and the Phoenicians?" friends ask and there is no simple answer. What is it about these ancient residents of what we now call the Levant who built landmarks for David and Solomon a thousand years before Jesus and were best known to the ancient Greeks as pirates? Well, I do love their enigmatic and contradictory trajectory across history: Semitic Asians who turn up in Greece and Italy at the right time to make a major contribution to the development of western civilisation; they're open-hearted, open-handed citizens of the world but some trade in slaves and at least a few sacrifice their own children; they're popularisers of the alphabet who left little of their own literature; they're artisans who steal from the best but with their own quirky style; they are mostly relegated to the footnotes of history but they occasionally jump out of ancient books to achieve astounding feats of navigation, trade and adventure then disappear in violent conflagrations or drift away into the mists of time. The Phoenicians did not exist in their own terms – the Greeks named them as such, mostly for propaganda purposes – yet they left a trail of objects, language and genes that attest to their vitality, vision and vast influence across time, across the Mediterranean and far beyond.

This book is not like any other. In more than 50 sonnets below, I sketch key locales along the Phoenician trading routes as well as weaving in other relevant stories and details of their trade: from trinkets, wares and commodities to myths and ideas. There are many footnotes supporting my contentious claims and suggesting further reading and my own simple illustrations of their alphabet and relevant maps and objects seeking to bring the story alive.

## The Phoenician Sonnets

This project started life as a footnote in my PhD thesis referring to a throwaway line in a *Scientific American* article that suggested the possibility of democracy in the Middle East before Athens 'invented' it. A decade later while stumbling around the Greek island of Chios, unsuccessfully seeking the site of the forum suggested on its constitution stone, I became aware of the island's contact with Phoenician traders in the Orientalising period (about 750-650 BCE) just before Chios became the site of one of the first experiments in Greek democracy. For some time, the possibility of the transmission of democratic ideas from the east to the west was a few squiggles on my whiteboard and then a very inquisitive PhD student, Ben Isakhan, now a professor at Deakin University, demanded an explanation. I admitted that in the aftermath of 9/11, I was intrigued by the possibility that the democracy George W. Bush contrived to defend in the War on Terror was a global, not a western idea, that democracy was older, more complex and more widely distributed than its traditional history allows.

From our discussions emerged our co-edited book *The Secret History of Democracy* which argued that perhaps democracy did not appear fully formed in Greece 2,600 years ago but rather it developed from prototypes in Asia, Africa and other unexpected places before and since its truly remarkable Greek iteration. One of my contributions to that book was a chapter sketching the development of proto-democratic institutions in the ancient Levant and how democracy may have been brought to Europe in nascent form by the archetypal Middle Eastern middlemen, the Phoenicians.

In 2010 while researching that chapter I travelled along the Phoenician trading routes from Carthage in Tunisia through Sicily, Southern Italy and Greece to Rhodes, Southern Turkey and Cyprus and on to Lebanon and Syria. In 2014 I travelled along their trading routes in the western Mediterranean to Rome, Sardinia, France, Spain, Portugal and Morocco to gather more material. In 2016 I had the opportunity to study collections of Phoenician

*Preface*

materials in museums in Berlin, Paris and London. When I retired from academia after that trip I had a large manuscript exploring the Phoenician trading routes, their trade and their ideas. I had the notion of completing a travel guide to high academic standards that also made the argument for the centrality of the Phoenicians in the spread of knowledge, ideas, enlightenment and civilisation.

In the early years of retirement, the manuscript kept growing like topsy as I focussed on different aspects of their trading routes and responded to the burgeoning academic literature on the Phoenicians. I also had an amusing variety of health issues that put off completion – aortic valve replacement, endocarditis, Parkinson's disease. But most disruptive was a growing interest in poetry, particularly long-form narratives re-imagining historical events like Magellan's doomed attempt to circumnavigate the planet and Allen Ginsberg's intervention that resulted in Ezra Pound recanting his anti-Semitism. In 2021 I published the products of this work in *The Voyage and the Vision*.

Buoyed by the enthusiasm for this kind of history, and thinking like a Phoenician, I realised there was another path for my metastasizing manuscript: it could avoid becoming like Walter Benjamin's giant, unfinished *Arcades Project* and metamorphose into something short, sweet and beautiful. Thus, I began writing the sonnets you have before you in the hope of producing something as intriguing as the Phoenicians themselves. Have I succeeded in this unlikely pursuit after thirty years of contemplation and work? You are the judge. I just hope that the Phoenicians would have liked it.

In my early research, I was greatly assisted by the advice of established scholars in the area such as Paulo Xella, Ida Oggiano and Giuseppe Garbati (Istituto di Studi sul Mediterraneo Antico, CNR, Rome), Jose Angel Zamora Lopez (Instituto de Lenguas y Culturas del Mediterráneo y Oriente Próximo, CCHS, Madrid) and Paloma Bueno Serrano (Universidad de Cadiz). Also of great assistance were the many people I met along the way who shared their knowledge

*The Phoenician Sonnets*

of their particular areas including Dr Salvatore Carboni in Cagliari and Dr Lucia Millas in Malaga and the intrepid drivers who got us to many obscure places, Mr Mazen in Lebanon and Syria, Chaair Abdellatif in Morocco and Omar Abu Sbeih in Israel and the Palestinian Territories. Thanks to my readers who provided many useful corrections and insights: Claudia Sagona, Stephanie Green, Ian Hutchesson and John C. Scott – errors remain my own. Many thanks to Professor Kay Ferres and Griffith University for the time to research this book and to my wife, Ann Baillie who has been most supportive of the project and in our travels to difficult and sometimes dangerous locales.

Stephen Stockwell
Burleigh Heads
2023

## Notes on Terminology

'Phoenician' is a loose term invented by the Greeks and applied by them to an amorphous group of traders and craftsmen from the east over an uncertain period. Its murky origins are discussed below. At its minimum, the term includes only the residents of Arwad, Byblos, Sidon and Tyre between 1100 and 332 BCE. At its maximum 'Phoenician' might include all those on the Mediterranean littoral between Ugarit in Syria and Dor in Israel/Palestine and some beyond including residents of Phoenician settlements in Cyprus, Carthage and many other colonies plus itinerant merchants and tradesmen moving about and living individually or in enclaves in other people's towns from 1600 BCE to well into the Christian era. I tend towards a maximalist position because it captures the breadth of the Phoenician enterprise.

Then there is 'Punic', the Roman word for Phoenician that has become roughly synonymous with 'Carthaginian' and includes not just the people of Carthage in Tunisia but also residents of their many colonies in the Western Mediterranean and beyond. For general purposes I use the term Phoenician, saving Carthaginian for when the context explicitly demands it. Sometimes common usage dictates Punic, for example, in reference to the Punic Wars and sometimes 'Punic' just fits the rhythm.

On matters poetic, I call these verses sonnets and they do adhere to the expected 14-line structure but their rhymes are a mix of formal patterns (Petrarchan, Shakespearean and Spenserian) depending on the subject matter. On rhythm, I have foregone the traditional iambic pentameter for the iambic hexameter which not only gives more space to the narrative, but also allows some use of the Alexandrine. Breaking all the rules, I conclude each sonnet with a line of iambic heptameter. Traditionalists will be askance but I hope the poems rock on by themselves.

I use BCE to denote dates 'before the common era', the equivalent of BC 'before Christ' and CE, 'common era' for ancient dates that once would have been described as AD. Dates of books and events from the modern period I leave unadorned.

# Chronology

(All dates are Before Common Era (BCE) and approximate)

*3500-2000 Early Bronze Age*
2750 Traditional founding date of Tyre

*2000-1550 Middle Bronze Age*
1800 'Proto-Canaanite' alphabetic script emerges in Egypt
1650-1550 Semitic Hyksos rule lower Egypt as the fifteenth dynasty

*1550-1200 Late Bronze Age (aka Greek Heroic Age)*
1360-1332 Amarna Letters

*1200-776 Iron Age (Dark Age in Greece aka Geometric Period)*
1200 Destruction of Ugarit by Sea People
1100 Tiglath-Pileser I of Assyria invades Canaan
1050 22-letter Phoenician alphabet in use in Byblos
1000 Tyre opens trade routes to western Mediterranean
950 Construction of Solomon's Temple
814 Traditional founding date of Carthage
800 Nora Stone

*776-538 Archaic Age (begins with the Orientalising Period to c. 650)*
750-725 Homer writes *Iliad* and *Odyssey*
662 Tyre rebels against Assyrians
585-572 Babylonians besiege Tyre
564-556 Non-monarchical judges govern Tyre

# Chronology

***538-332 Persian Period (roughly corresponds to the Classical Age in Greece)***
535 Battle of Alalia: Phoenician-Etruscan alliance defeats Greeks at sea off Corsica
508 Kleisthenes' reforms bring democracy to Athens
480 Battle of Salamis: Greeks defeat Persians and their Phoenician navy
    Battle of Himera: Syracuse defeats Carthage in Sicily
397 Syracuse destroys Motya
359-347 Tyre rebels against Persians

***332-64 Hellenistic Period*** (starts when Alexander the Great conquers Phoenicia)
264-241 First Punic War ends when Carthage loses the Battle of the Egadi Islands off Sicily
218-201 Second Punic War: Hannibal has success in Italy but loses war
150-146 Third Punic War ends with destruction of Carthage

*The Phoenician Sonnets*

# Introduction

*The Phoenician Sonnets*

Phoenician
9–8 Cent BCE, Dor

*Introduction*

**Who were the Phoenicians?**

Arwad, Byblos, Beirut, Sidon and fabled Tyre,
They're ports along the Mediterranean East,
That three millennia ago did explore and aspire
With Baal, their god, to trade to earth's far ends at least.

So timber, tin and trinkets, purple cloth and gold,
Glass flasks of sweet perfume, amphorae full of wine,
Whatever pleased a taste or met a need they sold,
Their drinking bowls bewitched,[1] their ivory work was fine.

To Greeks they're Phoenicians, blind Homer gave them fame,[2]
But to no nation bound, they praised their city's name.
Defeated much in war, their towns and cities burnt,
We know not much of them or how their glory's earnt.
So gird your loins and tightly tie your cloak and boots
And join our journey 'long the old Phoenician trading routes.

---

1 Glenn Markoe (1985) *Phoenician Bronze and Silver Bowls from Cyprus and the Mediterranean* Berkeley: University of California Press.
2 The first use of the term Phoenician is in Homer (c. 750 BCE) *The Iliad* at XXIII.744: *phoinikes* means 'crimson people' which comes from *phoinós*, 'blood red'. The Greeks may have been referring to the Phoenicians ruddy complexions or the reddish-purple cloth they brought for trade. *Phoinix* also means 'date palm' and is the name of the legendary immortal bird that keeps rising from its own ashes but any links between those meanings and the traders are more obscure. The term 'Phoenician' may have deeper roots in the Bronze Age Mycenaean *po-ni-ki-jo* ('crimson'/'date palm'), perhaps derived from the Ancient Egyptian *fenkhu* meaning people from Canaan and beyond (Françoise Briquel-Chatonnet & Eric Gubel (1999) *Les Phéniciens: Aux origines du Liban* Paris: Gallimard: 18).

*The Phoenician Sonnets*

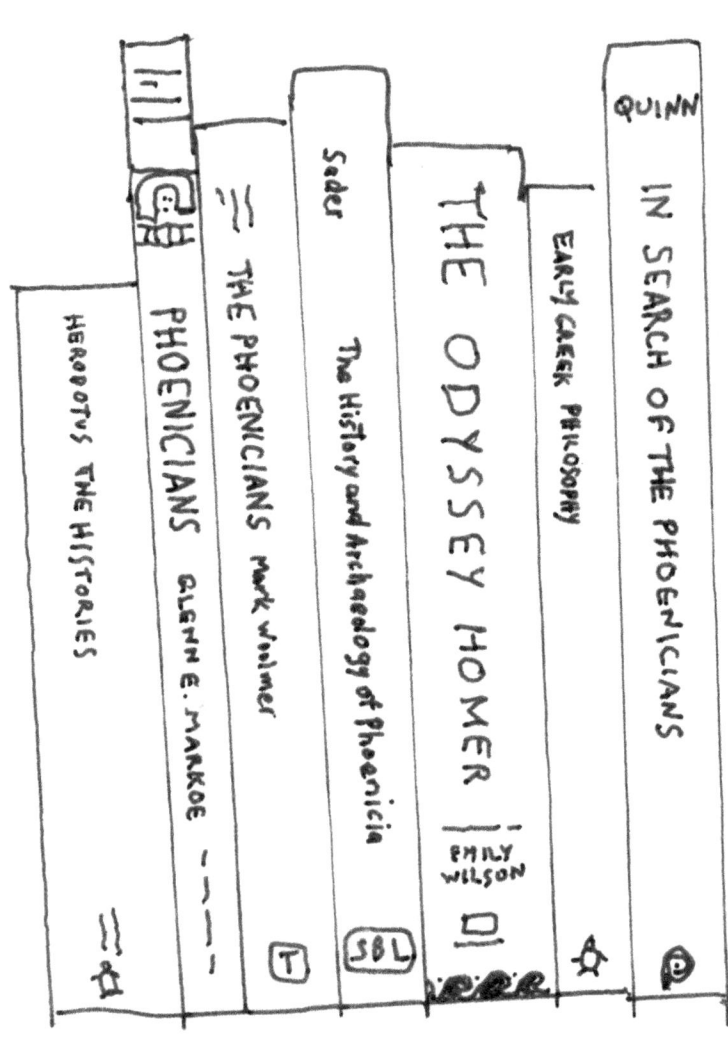

# Introduction

## Sources

Phoenicians were ill-served by their own stationery
Josephus knew their archives,[3] others read their books,[4]
But those papyrus texts were burnt by enemy[5]
Or worm and rot have left just scraps and fleeting looks.

Greeks: Homer, Herodotus and Thucydides[6]
Mix praise for Phoenicians with some propaganda,
In Roman times: Strabo, Pliny and Plutarch please,[7]
They deal in facts without spin or slimy slander.

The Bible's bias shows but from Genesis to
Ezekiel slowly Phoenician details accrue.
Digs found clay texts in Amarna[8] and Ugarit[9]
And Assyrian annals and reliefs help bits fit.[10]
More comes from archaeology that's prolific
And work with language, genes and advances scientific.[11]

---

3 Flavius Josephus (c. 100 CE) *Against Apion* I.20.
4 Pherecydes of Syros (c. 580-520 BCE) "is said to have had no teacher, but to have used… the 'secret books of the Phoenicians'", M.L. West (1971) *Early Greek Philosophy and the Orient* Oxford: Clarendon Press: 1-3. Philo of Byblos (c. 64-141 CE) acknowledges the books of the ancient Phoenician writer, Sanchuniathon, see Albert I. Baumgarten (1981) *The Phoenician History of Philo of Byblos* Leiden: Brill: 6-7.
5 Many libraries, books and records were likely destroyed in Alexander the Great's sack of Tyre in 332 BCE and Rome's destruction of Carthage in 146 BCE.
6 Homer's *The Iliad* and (c. 725 BCE) *The Odyssey* have positive references to Sidonians but are mostly negative on Phoenicians. Herodotus (c. 430 BCE) *The Histories* celebrates Tyre but blames Phoenicians for the kidnappings that led to the Trojan War. Thucydides (c. 410 BCE) *History of the Peloponnesian War* casts Phoenicians as pirates.
7 Strabo (c. 24 CE) *The Geography*, Pliny the Elder (c. 77 CE) *The Natural History*, Plutarch (c. 100 CE) *Parallel Lives*.
8 W.L. Moran (ed) (1992) *The Amarna Letters*, Baltimore: Johns Hopkins University Press.
9 Manfried Dietrich et al (eds) (1995) *The Cuneiform Alphabetic Texts* Munster: Ugarit-Verlag.
10 A.K. Grayson (2000) *Assyrian and Babylonian Chronicles* Winona Lake: Eisenbrauns. Important reliefs are documented in Glenn Markoe (2000) *Phoenicians* London: The British Museum Press: 38, 41, 44-5, 47.
11 For a recent overview of an integrated, scientific archaeology of the Phoenician homeland, see Helene Sader (2019) *The History and Archaeology of Phoenicia* Atlanta: SBL Press.

*Introduction*

**Chios**

Our story starts half way, the Greek isle of Chios,
My wife and son and I, we come in hope of spring
But meet cold, wintry winds, and I am at a loss:
How daunting is my search for where free speech begins?

Its Constitution Stone gave old Chios renown,[12]
Claiming its people's council ruled as Athens' stirred,[13]
But where did democracy first meet in this town?
Then in the local museum I heard the word:[14]

That Phoenicians had visited in times remote
And left Chios their image of a female sphinx,[15]
And too, I thought, a start: free speech and open vote
As I recalled notions touching on Eastern links
To young democracy in Bernal's books[16]… and thus
Began my trail along their route, writ in this Periplus.[17]

---

12  T. Meiggs & D. Lewis (eds) (1988) *Greek Historical Inscriptions* Oxford: Clarendon Press: 14.
13  L.H. Jeffery (1956) 'The courts of Justice in archaic Chios' *Annual of the British School at Athens 51*: 157-167.
14  Chios Archaeological Museum, visited 2002.
15  A. Archontidou-Argyri & T. Kyriakopoulou (eds) (2000) *Chios – Oinopion's Town* Chios: Ministry of Culture: 18-20.
16  Starting with Martin Bernal (1991) *Black Athena: The Afroasiatic Roots of Classical Civilisation, Volume I: The Fabrication of Ancient Greece 1785-1985* London: Vintage: 22 and then pursued in some detail in his 2001 'Phoenician Politics and Egyptian Justice in Ancient Greece' *Black Athena Writes Back: Martin Bernal responds to his critics* Durham: Duke University Press: 345-372.
17  A periplus is an aid to navigation that logs the towns and landmarks along a coast with notes of geographical, political and social highlights. See for example Hanno (c. 400 BCE) *The Periplus of Hanno*.

*The Phoenician Sonnets*

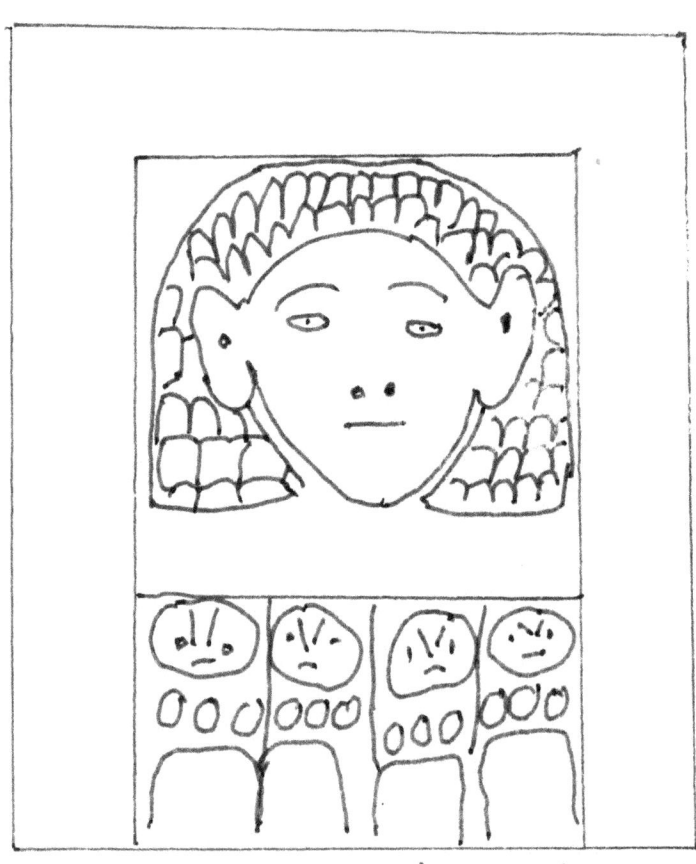

Ivory Woman at the Window

*Introduction*

## History

You'll find the Phoenicians buried in footnotes deep:[18]
They're pirates, thieves and tricksters who could turn their hand
To sailing boats and trade and crafts upon the land.
Born coastal Canaanites, they're caught in history's sweep

When fifteen hundred years before Christ's time they found
Themselves between warlike Hittites and Egyptians,
Then Sea Peoples came to give those states conniptions
And Phoenician folk found freedom on their home ground.

They'd been across the sands to Mesopotamia
Now they sailed west to Cyprus, on to Crete and Greece,
Then Sicily, Tunis, Sardinia, Iberia
And founded towns still there like Carthage[19] and Cadiz.
They listened carefully and learnt from those they met
And spread some big ideas like fine art and the alphabet.

---

18 For a magisterial introduction to the Phoenicians' history, even if it is a little dated and overly enthusiastic to proclaim Phoenician nationhood, it is hard to beat Sabatino Moscati (ed) (1988) *The Phoenicians* Milan: Bompiani. A briefer account incorporating more recent research and contemporary thinking is provided by Mark Woolmer (2017) *A Short History on the Phoenicians* London: I.B. Tauris. The most comprehensive account of the Phoenicians is given by Markoe *Phoenicians* either the 2000 original from the British Museum or the 2005 reprint lovingly published by The Folio Society.
19 Though the Romans destroyed Carthage in 146 BCE and Gaius Gracchus tried and failed to re-establish it in 122 BCE, it was re-founded by Emperor Augustus Caesar in 29 BCE and continues to flourish today.

*The Phoenician Sonnets*

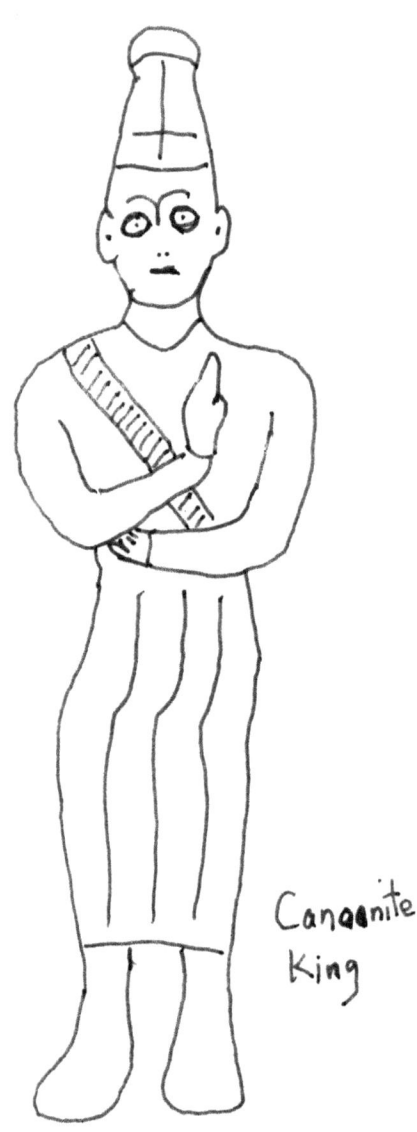

*Introduction*

## Canaan

Canaanite culture rose four thousand years ago,
In Levantine walled towns fed by pastoral tribes
Like Ugarit, Byblos, Hazor and Jericho,
They pioneered trade routes and had inventive scribes.[20]

Kings in cone crowns ruled with pomegranate sceptres,
El and Asherah lead a brood of fractious gods,
Folk made jewels, snakes and masks for their sacred sectors,
Their culture kept independent against all odds.[21]

Some settled in Egypt and became Hyksos kings,
The story of Joseph's coat may touch on these things[22]
And forced to flee did they wander for forty years
Before returning to Phoenicia and their peers?[23]
Canaan was broad enough for many different kinds,
O, that all its diverse children now find a peace that binds.

---

20 Canaanites had many similarities to their Phoenician descendants and can be described as 'proto Phoenician', see Ann E. Killebrew (2019) 'Canaanite Roots, Proto Phoenicia, and Early Phoenicia: ca. 1300-1000 BCE' in Brian R. Doak & Carolina López-Ruiz (eds) *The Oxford Handbook of the Phoenician and Punic Mediterranean* Oxford: Oxford University Press: 39-55.
21 This material was gathered at the Israel Museum, Jerusalem (visited 2022).
22 Genesis 37-59.
23 Including nations such as the Ammon, Moab and Edom. Genetic research indicates that residents of Israel, Palestine and Lebanon share Canaanite heritage, see Andrew Lawler (2020) 'DNA from the Bible's Canaanites lives on in modern Arabs and Jews' *National Geographic* 29 May.

## The Phoenician Sonnets

*Introduction*

## Mesopotamia

Twixt Euphrates and Tigris, the first cities grow,
Rich, watered soil turns farms to empires with writing.
They win the north then west, their army is on show,
Phoenicians swap tribute for trade and shun fighting.[24]

Assyrians come for cedar, but with no remorse,
Take back metal, monkeys and ivories finely made.
Next comes Nebuchadnezzar, Babylon's strong force,
Tough Tyre holds out for years then does a deal for trade.[25]

Phoenicians play the game to bring wealth from the east
In caravans piled high, on the humped desert beast,
Lapis lazuli, spice, carpets, fabrics of silk,
But best was knowledge borne by students and their ilk,
Mathematics, literature and astronomy,
Things that improve the mind and soul, and the economy.[26]

---

24 At the start of the eleventh century BCE, Markoe *Phoenicians*: 26.
25 The siege of Tyre was 585-572 BCE, ibid: 47.
26 In 2010 there was still an ancient sign in the old caravanserai in Palmyra offering tax breaks for caravans accompanied by a scholar.

# Homeland

*The Phoenician Sonnets*

*Homeland*

## Ugarit

Ugarit was gone before Phoenicians found fame,
Yet like them traded metal, glass and purple dyes.
They had an early alphabet and praised Baal's name
And from their coastal city state sought enterprise.[27]

The diggings show they're Phoenician or much the same:[28]
Five thousand clay tablets tell how they organised
City affairs and trade, crops, horses, fish and game;
Plus myths, star charts and songs to gods they idolised.[29]

A thousand years they thrived, their art and music charmed
But all that changed fast when the Sea Peoples appeared
And cracked the city while their troops were far away[30]
And though their civilisation was sorely harmed
Their story came back to life when the site was cleared
And standing in their ruins, we felt those folk alive today.

---

27 A simple but comprehensive guide to the history and archaeology of the site: Jamal Haydar (2009) *Ugarit* Lattakia: Almersat.
28 While some argue that Ugarit was geographically 'out of Phoenicia proper' (Markoe *Phoenicians*: 16) and 'pre-dates the traditional period of Phoenician history by 200 years' (Woolmer *A Short History*: 17) others point to the traces, links and continuities from Ugarit to the Phoenician cities (S.F. Bondi 1988 'The Origins in the East' in Moscati *The Phoenicians*: 35). Given that Phoenicia was never a formal nation state but a Greek invention after Ugarit flourished beside similar sister cities such as Byblos and Tyre which are regarded as Phoenician, it seems churlish to exclude Ugarit from the Phoenician panoply.
29 Dietrich et al *The Cuneiform Alphabetic Texts*.
30 As suggested by the Ugarit cuneiform tablet translated in M. Cooke, E. Goknar & G. Parker (eds) (2008) *Mediterranean Passages* Chapel Hill: University of North Carolina Press: 18.

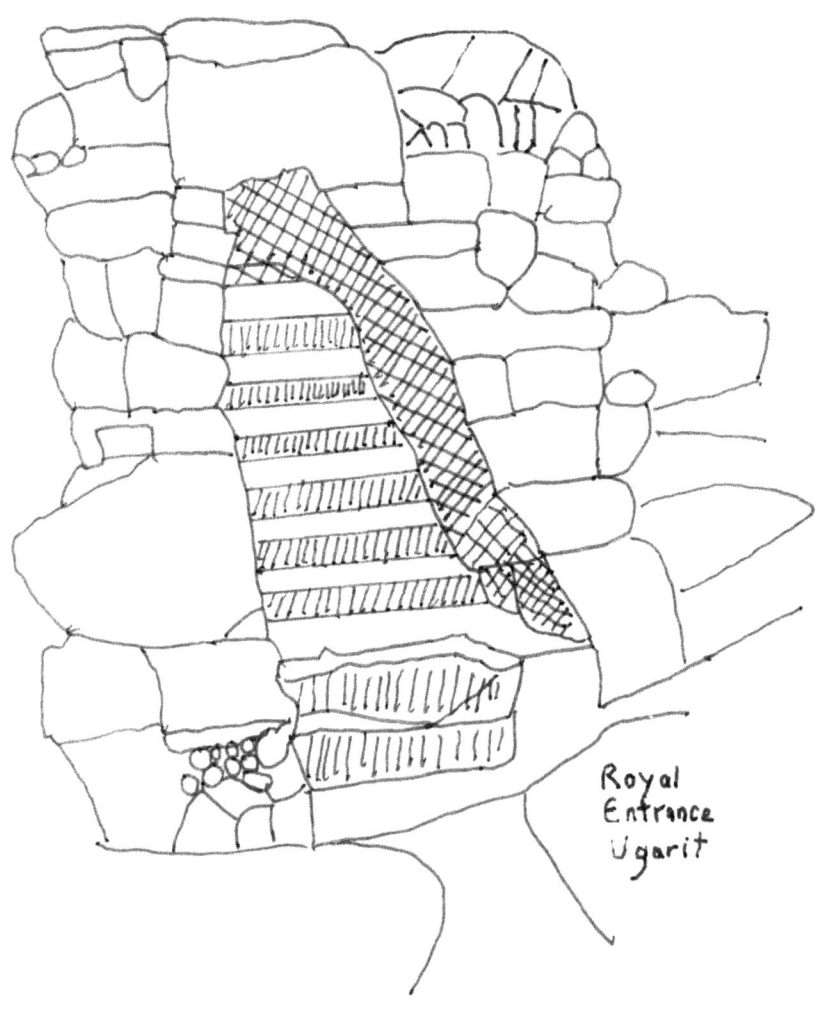

## Sea Peoples

The late Bronze Age saw Eastern palace states well-fed
But quakes and climate change brought famine and revolt[31]
And warrior bands stalking sea and land – spreading dread
From Troy to Ugarit, looting without a halt.

With origins obscure but dress distinct they're called
Sea Peoples but they're many tribes: Tjeker, Sherden
And fearsome Philistines – they destroy cities walled[32]
But some Phoenician towns do not bear this burden.[33]

In Egypt's Delta Ramses turns them back with cost,
The battle's won with glory but his throne's soon lost.
As palaces fall so power shifts and trade is freed,
The Phoenicians do deals and sow some social seed,
Sea Peoples settle south, pot sherds tell the story,[34]
They work together on trade and travels exploratory.

---

31 B.L. Drake (2012) 'The influence of climatic change on the Late Bronze Age Collapse and the Greek Dark Ages' *Journal of Archaeological Science* 39(6): 1862-1870.
32 The existence of the Sea People is much debated. Like the Phoenicians they were a disparate group named by others, Egyptians in this case. What can be said is that the collapse of palatial cultures at the end of the Bronze Age was accompanied by unruly migrations and much destruction. For a detailed account, see Eric H. Cline (2014) *1177 B.C.: The Year Civilization Collapsed* Princeton: Princeton University Press.
33 Markoe *Phoenicians*: 23-25 but he does not give a compelling reason why the Phoenician cities were spared, nor does anyone else.
34 Ayelet Gilboa (2005) 'Sea Peoples and Phoenicians along the Southern Phoenician Coast—A Reconciliation: An Interpretation of Šikila (SKL) Material Culture' *Bulletin of the American Schools of Oriental Research* 337:47–78, contextualized again in her (2022) 'The Southern Levantine Roots of the Phoenician Mercantile Phenomenon', *BASOR* 387: 31-53.

*The Phoenician Sonnets*

*Homeland*

**Arwad**

Arwad's an island port, close to the Syrian coast,
Spring fed so safe from siege,[35] with links east through Homs Gap,
Across the desert, past Palmyra, to silk roads
And rich cities on the Mesopotamian map.

Their caravans and boats brought Arwad confidence,
From early times the people there sought sovereignty.[36]
When Assyria invades and times are most intense,
Arwad trades fragrant wood to keep Phoenicians free.[37]

Six years after I travelled there I came back to life,
Technically I'd been dead under the surgeon's knife.
Awake I rejoice in the glittering, shimmering light
And recall seeing Arwad in a sea that bright,
Happy with those people, that freedom-loving flock,
Who prize their independence as they cling tight to their rock.

---

35 Strabo *The Geography*: XVI.2.13 tells of Arwadi folk harvesting fresh water from springs beneath the sea.
36 The Egyptian Amarna Letters (c. 1360-1332 BCE) show the democratic inclinations of the 'people of Arwad' when they're reported engaging in action against the pharaoh, most particularly when 'Zimredda of Sidon, the rebel against the pharaoh, and the men of Arwad have exchanged oaths among themselves, and they have assembled their ships, chariots and infantry, to capture Tyre, the maidservant of the pharaoh' (Moran *The Amarna Letters*: #101, #105, #149). This rebellion, however brief, is evidence for 'the people, as opposed to the monarch, as sovereign' (Bernal *Black Athena Writes Back*: 356-357).
37 Around 1110 BCE the Assyrian king, Tiglath-Pileser I, invaded Canaan to gather the cedar required for temple renovations in Ashur and Arwad took the lead in negotiations and delivery of the timber in a manner that maintained the independence of what would become the 'Phoenician' cities (Markoe *Phoenicians*: 26).

*The Phoenician Sonnets*

Baal in Louvre Museum

*Homeland*

## Religion

El's father of the gods, Asherah's fertile mum,
Baal matters most, the weather god helps crops to soar
And sailors pray to him for wind so coasts will come,
His wife is Astarte, goddess of love and war.[38]

Bes helps women survive, Reshef deals with disease,
While Sahar and Salem ensure the dusk and dawn.[39]
Each town has their own Baal, Byblos hails Adonis,
Tyre: Melqart, Sidon: Eshmun, each year they're reborn.[40]

The gods were specialised, it's something very odd
As Jonah says, in storms: 'each cried to his own god'.[41]
In Carthage Baal Hammon was king, Tanit his queen,
But people had a rite we see as quite obscene:
Some sacrificed their children for the gods' pleasure,
The tophets sad today, still haunted by their lost treasure.[42]

---

38 Baal was often connected to thunder like the Greek god Zeus, while Astarte, often the preeminent partner in the relationship, has many similarities to the Greek goddess Aphrodite.
39 Markoe *Phoenicians:* 124-125; Sergio Ribichini (1988) 'Beliefs and Religious Life' in Moscati *The Phoenicians:* 106; Haydar *Ugarit:* 36.
40 Baal's power over the weather grew to include nature's cycles and he was invoked to ensure the return of the seasons: see Markoe *Phoenician:* 116-119.
41 Jonah 1:5. See also A.J. Brody (1999) *Each Man Cried Out to his God: The Specialized Religion of Canaanite and Phoenician Seafarers* Atlanta: Scholars Press.
42 Tophets are children's graveyards at Carthaginian sites in Tunisia, Sicily and Sardinia. While some children were clearly sacrificed, many may have died of natural causes. See further discussion in 'Tophets' below.

*The Phoenician Sonnets*

*Homeland*

## Byblos

Perched high on a headland with a perennial spring
Byblos, ancient Gebal, has many tales to tell:
Two temples to the gods, two ports that great wealth bring,
They're in the copper trade with cedar trees to fell.[43]

Though caught in Egypt's thrall, rebellion's always there,[44]
Once free the king rules with the city's assembly,[45]
So when the priest from Egypt comes with just a prayer
To flee the pirates' rage, to council he must plea.[46]

For a thousand years Byblos steers its own sweet way
Through trouble and invasion, tribute it would pay
To then become the seat of administration.[47]
Early adopter of alphabetization[48]
And then the literate heart of the papyrus trade,[49]
Thank Byblos whenever a bibliography is made!

---

43 Markoe *Phoenicians*: 202.
44 The local king of Byblos complains to the pharaoh: 'I am afraid the peasantry will strike me down... A man with a bronze dagger attacked... I was struck nine times. Accordingly, I fear for my life' (Moran *The Amarna Letters*: #77, #81). These passages suggest an independent-minded citizenry with some degree of internal cohesion and organisation. Flinders Petrie identifies 'people from Gubla (Byblos)' communicating directly with the pharaoh in his (1898) *Syria and Egypt* London: Methuen: 99.
45 Ezekiel 27:9 refers to this assembly as 'the ancients of Gebal [Byblos] and the wise men thereof'.
46 H. Goedicke (1975) *The Report of Wenamun* Baltimore: John Hopkins University Press: 123. This papyrus has a colourful provenance and is now appreciated as a work of literature but it gives much context to the Eastern Mediterranean in the early Iron Age. Initially the text's hieroglyphic for 'assembly' resisted translation but it has now been transcribed as *mu'd* which is close to the Hebrew word for assembly, *mo'ed*, see J.A. Wilson (1945) 'The Assembly of a Phoenician City' *Journal of Near Eastern Studies* 4(4): 245.
47 For example, in the Persian period 538-332 BCE, see Markoe *Phoenicians*: 203.
48 Markoe *Phoenicians*: 109-111.
49 Lorenzo Nigro (2020) 'Byblos, an ancient capital of the Levant' *Revue Phénicienne* 100 Spécial: 61.

# The Phoenician Sonnets

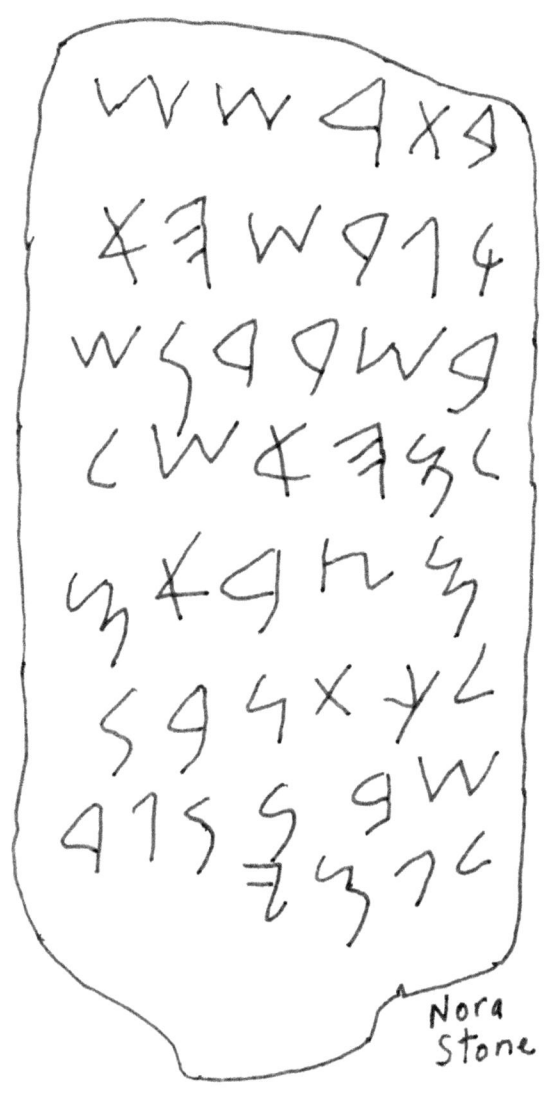

*Homeland*

## Alphabet

The alphabet is such a cunning, canny tool[50]
And to the Canaanites we owe a literary debt:
For sounds, they used the signs that hieroglyphics set
And dropped signs for whole words that were so hard to school

Which left just letters that most could quite quickly learn,
A democratic spell from those Egypt oppressed.[51]
In Ugarit cuneiform letters sounds expressed,[52]
But Byblos found sound symbols easy to discern.[53]

Phoenicians spread the word, the Nora Stone attests,[54]
The Greeks then added vowels and alphabets went on
To Rome and Spain, then northern runes and far beyond.[55]
We use them still when minds are blurred and thoughts are pests,
From alphabetical order to Ikea kits[56]
Those little letters work to make sure that everything fits.

---

50 The McLuhanite argument for the contribution of the alphabet to abstract and analytic thought and thus western civilisation is summarised in R.K. Logan (2004) *The Alphabet Effect* Cresskill: Hampton Press. Its ethno-centric bias has been criticised though the alphabet's systematising effects remain apparent.
51 The earliest examples of the 'proto-Canaanite' alphabetic script have been found near Luxor, Egypt and date to 1800 BCE. Slightly later examples have been found in the Sinai, see Woolmer *A Short History:* 79, Markoe *Phoenicians:* 110-111, 114.
52 Markoe *Phoenicians:* 111. In the excavation of Ugarit, a small clay tablet was found (measuring 5.5 x 1.3 cm) that appears to be a learning aid to help students memorise the alphabet (Haydar *Ugarit:* 22). The original can be seen in the Damascus National Museum, visited 2008 and 2010.
53 Around 1050 BCE, if not earlier: Woolmer *A Short History:* 79-80.
54 The Nora Stone found in Sardinia has been dated to c. 800 BCE. For more detail, see 'Sardinia' below.
55 Re runes see Robert Mailhammer & Theo Vennemann (2019) *The Carthaginian North: Semitic influence on early Germanic* Amsterdam: John Benjamins.
56 For more on the early use of matching letters in the construction of pre-fabricated kits, see the discussion under 'Ships' below.

*The Phoenician Sonnets*

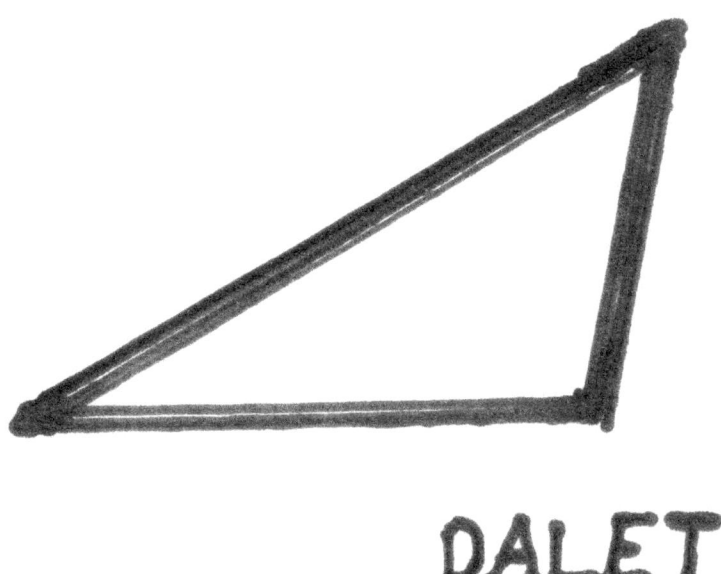

*Homeland*

**Beirut**

Beirut's a bustling town, tensions always bubbling,
An ancient city port, long a seat of learning.
It bears the scars of war, melted treasures troubling,
The National Museum has survived much burning:[57]

Stone gods and arrowheads from the Neolithic
Now sit beside Bronze Age bulls and gilded statues
With ivory ducks and deer, they've powers terrific
As do the masks and jewels, and bards who sing the news.[58]

These things from Phoenicia influenced further west
As did script on the sarcophagus of Hiram.[59]
Down along the Corniche, we see in peoples' eyes
Something else they sent west to help with life's tough test,
Like Phoenicians who went forth, when hard times try them,
Beirutis have the strength stoic philosophy supplies.[60]

---

57 During the Lebanese Civil War (1975-90), The National Museum was on the 'Green Line' between warring parties and much of the collection was destroyed though, due to the bravery of the Museum staff, many important objects survive. We visited there in 2010.
58 National Museum of Lebanon (2008) *A visit to the Museum* Beirut: Ministry of Culture.
59 Originally from the Royal Tombs of Byblos, dated to the 10$^{th}$ century BCE, this sarcophagus has one of the earliest inscriptions in the Phoenician language: NMOL *A visit to the Museum*: 30-31.
60 Did Phoenicians invent stoicism? See more on Zeno, the founder of stoic philosophy under 'Kition' below.

*The Phoenician Sonnets*

Cedar of Lebanon

*Homeland*

## Cedar

This mighty tree is known as *Cedrus Libani*,
An evergreen conifer in the pine family.
Its strong, fragrant timber was used in ancient time
For palaces and temples and boats fast and fine.

Assyrians came from far with troops to harvest it,[61]
Egyptians came each year and took all that would fit.[62]
And Hiram, king of Tyre sent David wood and men
To build his house[63] then Solomon said come again

To build the Temple of the Lord.[64] These trees were large,
One hundred and thirty feet tall, eight foot across.
Mile high they live, they're hard to handle to the barge.
At sea they'd shift, go overboard, the trader's loss
But our gain today as we see in the museum[65]
A massive piece of drift wood, its quality still premium.

---

61 Markoe *Phoenicians*: 26.
62 ibid: 19; Goedicke *The Report of Wenamun*.
63 2 Samuel 5:11.
64 1 Kings 5-7.
65 American University of Beirut Museum, visited 2010.

*The Phoenician Sonnets*

HE

*Homeland*

**Sidon to Sarepta**

The Bible says Sidon is first born of Canaan,[66]
Placed on a promontory, protected by a reef,
It battled Tyre and foreign foes, oft finding grief.[67]
The beauty of its craft, the breadth of its trading

Meant it soon returned with strategies astounding.[68]
Their favoured god, Eshmun, with staff and two winged snakes
Spread health across the lands, all maladies and breaks
Were healed at his temple, patients soon rebounding.[69]

Then south to Sarepta, an industrial city
Famed for its red-slip pots and amphorae for oil,
Its shrine to Astarte a monument to toil.[70]
Seeking the site, we almost found calamity,
On a quiet road, gunmen appear wildly waving,
Our driver guns the car away, it feels most life-saving.[71]

---

66 Genesis 10:15.
67 Markoe *Phoenicians:* 199-201.
68 When defeated on the coast, Sidon used its connections inland through the Beqaa Valley to rebuild its trade routes and flourished in Babylonian and Persian times providing health and naval services as well as finely crafted objects and garments.
69 Eshmun, Sidon's Baal, had powers and symbolic insignia similar to Asclepius, the Greek god of healing and the two were associated from 'very early on', around 1000 BCE: Ribichini 'Beliefs...': 110.
70 James Pritchard (1978) *Recovering Sarepta, A Phoenician City: excavations at Sarafand, Lebanon, 1969-1974* Princeton: Princeton University Press.
71 As we drove away from the headland near the Sarepta archaeological site, its strategic significance became apparent and we realised the well-armed men may have been security officials rather than kidnappers.

# The Phoenician Sonnets

Ivory Sphinx
Ashmolean Museum

*Homeland*

**Ivory**

Finely carved ivory was part of Phoenician trade.[72]
From local hippo teeth, elephants near and far,
They honed this precious stuff and jewels precisely made
To tell fantastic tales about creatures bizarre:[73]

Gryphons and sphinxes, ethereal spirits above
And from below, demons with intents infernal.
Plus women in the windows, goddesses of love,
And men with goats tend trees of life, hope eternal.

We find this ivory all along the trading route,
There are African tusks in shipwrecks[74] and workshops
And well-wrought treasures found in graves and as war loot.
Assyrians took it as tribute when they were tops,
Decorating furniture and cavalry steeds.
When found again we see, ivory's beauty fills human needs.

---

72 Ezekiel 27:15.
73 Markoe *Phoenicians* 46-47.
74 See, for example, the shipwreck found in Bajo de la Campana near the Spanish town of Murcia dated to 600 BCE carrying thirteen African elephant tusks, four engraved with Phoenician inscriptions: M.E. Aubet Semmler (2002) 'Phoenician trade in the West' in Marilyn R. Bierling (ed and trans) *The Phoenicians in Spain: an archaeological review of the eighth-sixth centuries B.C.E.* Winona Lake: Eisenbrauns: 106.

*The Phoenician Sonnets*

*Homeland*

## Tyre

Tyre's towers rose from seas, from shoals just off the coast,
Melqart's temple's columns gleamed gold and emerald bright.[75]
They guided merchants home, back from their trading posts,
Her sailors ruled the sea, they steered by stars at night.

Tyre traded east and west for metal, spice[76] and gold,
She bloomed in Hiram's time, he strutted the world stage,
But people rising up made Pygmalion so bold,
He usurped Dido's crown - she fled to found Carthage.[77]

War with Assyrian troops then undermines the king,[78]
When Babylon arrives, royals fall, mere men ruling:[79]
Then Alexander builds a ramp from coast to isle
That ends brave Tyre's freedoms in a most brutal style.
The town grew back in Roman and Crusader times
And still today it rocks with independent beats and rhymes.

---

75 Herodotus *The Histories* I.45.
76 A. Gilboa (2015) 'On the Beginnings of South Asian Spice Trade with the Mediterranean Region' *Radiocarbon* 5: 265–283.
77 G. Rawlinson (1889) *History of Phoenicia* London: Longmans, Green and Co: 205.
78 Tyre's treaty with the Assyrian Esarhaddon suggests the elder's council is an equal partner with the king: Markoe *Phoenicians:* 88.
79 Josephus *Against Apion*: I.21.

*The Phoenician Sonnets*

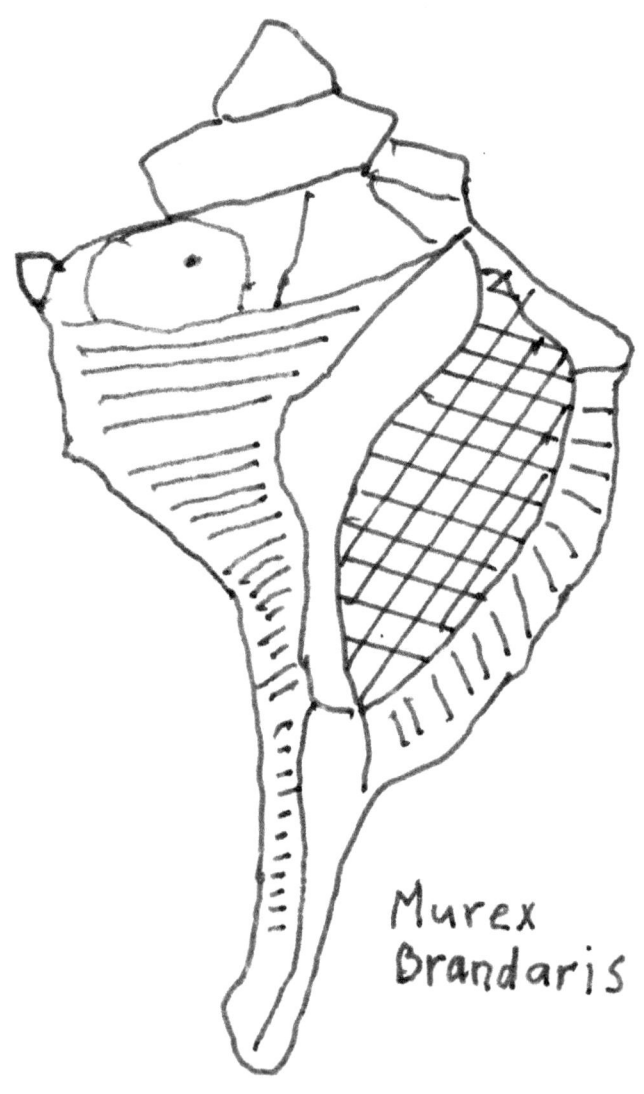

*Homeland*

## Purple

Greeks called them Phoenicians after their purple dye,
That's extracted from carnivorous Murex snails.[80]
Their process was secret and though other folk try
Phoenician brand's preferred, it's fast and never fails.

To make the dye the shell is cracked and gland cut out,
Its clear juices mixed with salt water and potash,
Exposed to sun and air, the right shades come about:[81]
Sidon's dye indigo, Tyre's had a blood red dash.

In myth the dye was found by Melqart by the sea,
His dog bit a snail shell, its mouth turned bright purple
His nymph said 'Dye my gown', so starts the industry.[82]
As Heracles, his works the middle sea circle,
His trail a purple thread from homeland to Maroc,[83]
Following Phoenician trading routes with beauty baroque.

---

80 Irving Ziderman (1990) 'Seashells and Ancient Purple Dyeing' *The Biblical Archaeologist* 53 (2): 98-101.
81 Pliny *The Natural History* IX.60-65.
82 Julius Pollux (c. 183 CE) *Onomasticon* I.45-49.
83 For an account that puts the Phoenician purple trade in Morocco at the very start of commerce in the Atlantic, see Simon Winchester (2010) *Atlantic* London: Harper: 66-68.

*The Phoenician Sonnets*

*Homeland*

## To Dor

Past Tyre, there's Akko where Sherden Sea People toiled,
Phoenicians came to trade and sing Asherah's praise[84]
And stayed to make things bronze and jars for wine and oil.
Then south to Dor where more Sea People passed their days -

The signs of Tjeker cults have been excavated:
Knives, bowls 'n' music maker from shoulder bone of bull.
Signs too that Phoenicians were well integrated,
Making glass, charms and amulets, their ships jammed full.[85]

And three millennia hence, Rothschild's Zionist dream
To bottle Hebrew wine on local folk looked down,
Ignored ecology so became a failed scheme.[86]
Then Israel's army came and massacred the town.[87]
The kibbutz fixed the ruins[88] but lessons were not learnt:
Integrate like the Phoenicians so peace is really earnt.[89]

---

84 Markoe *Phoenicians:* 193-194.
85 For an up to date account of what the pottery remains tell us about the development of Phoenician 'process' in the Southern Levant in the late second millennia BCE, see Gunnar Lehmann (2021) 'The Emergence of Early Phoenicia' *Jerusalem Journal of Archaeology* 1: 272-324 though Gilboa 'Sea Peoples and Phoenicians along the Southern Phoenician Coast' remains central in appreciating the cultural interaction in the area that benefitted both Sea Peoples and Phoenicians.
86 Originally built in 1891 as a glass bottle factory, the Zionist experiment was afflicted by malaria, unsuitable sand and debt and was wound up leaving the building to the mercy of the elements.
87 There is strong oral evidence from both sides that Israelis massacred 40-200 Palestinian Arabs at the village of Tantura near Tel Dor on 22–23 May 1948. Adam Raz (2022) 'There's a Mass Palestinian Grave at a Popular Israeli Beach, Veterans Confess' *Haaretz*, 20 January.
88 In the 1980s the Kibbutz Nahsholim restored Rothschild's glass bottle factory to house artefacts from the nearby Tel Dor excavations and created the HaMizgaga Museum of Archaeology and Glass, visited in 2022.
89 Let's hear it for the One State Solution where everyone forgives everyone and returned Palestinians become citizens and work with Israelis to make a wealthy, integrated, tolerant and democratic society. Crazy? Not as crazy as living in a warzone forever.

# The Phoenician Sonnets

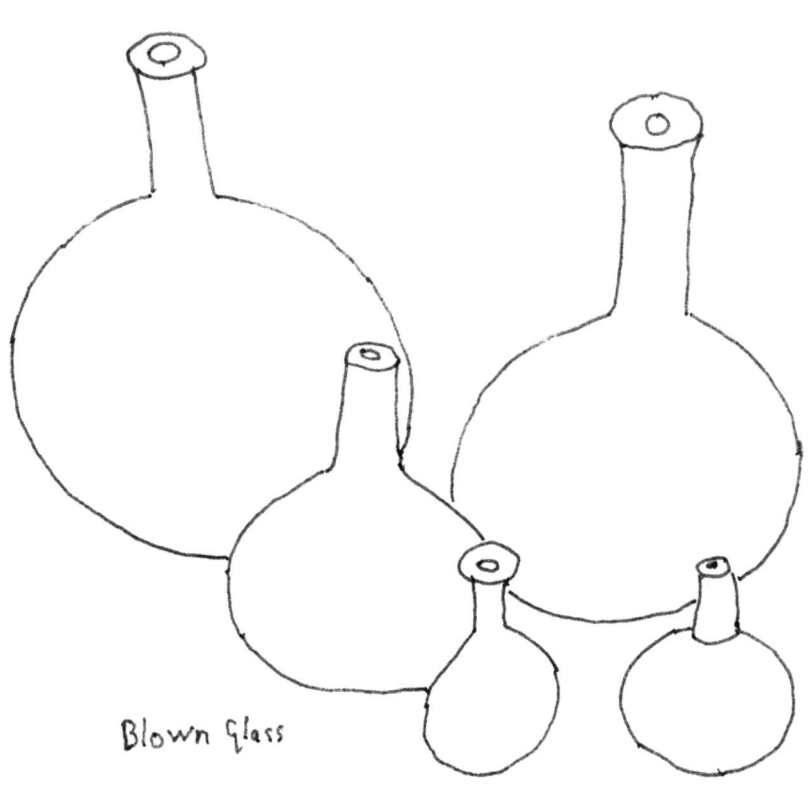

*Homeland*

**Glass**

As traders keen to catch the shopper's eye and purse,
The Phoenicians made much glittering, gleaming glass,
Sold from Spain to China,[90] it started world commerce,[91]
Thus Pliny thought that they first made glass come to pass.[92]

But 'twas techniques they took from Egypt and the East
That made their art alive in baubles, beads 'n' brooches:
They learnt that glass is made by melting sand at heat
With scientific and industrial approaches.[93]

They wound it round sand cores for jars and jugs and fish
And scary talismans as spooky as you wish.[94]
They ground it down for faience to make glistening things,[95]
Glass glamorous and glorious lifts us on its wings.
As their age was going, with embers aglowing,
It's Phoenicians who find the finer art of glass-blowing.[96]

---

90 Glenn Markoe (2000) 'Mediterranean Glass Eye Beads in China' in M.E. Aubet & M. Barthélemy (eds), *Actas del IV Congreso internacional de estudios fenicios y púnicos* Cádiz, 2-6 October 1995: 401-409.
91 See references to Bronze Age glass trade: with Egypt in Moran *Amarna Letters* #148, #235, #314, #323, #327 & #331; and further afield in shipwrecks discovered off the Turkish coast at Ulu Burun and Cape Gelidonya: George F. Bass (ed) (2005) *Beneath the Seven Seas* New York: Thames & Hudson.
92 Pliny *The Natural History*: XXXVI.65.
93 For a brief but passionate account of the practicalities of ancient glass-making, see Ralph Bruin (2007) 'Brilliant Glass *Archaeological Diggings* 14(1): 41-43.
94 Maria L. Uberti (1988) 'Glass' in Moscati *The Phoenicians*: 474-476.
95 Markoe *Phoenicians*: 158.
96 ibid: 156.

*The Phoenician Sonnets*

*Homeland*

**South**

The Philistines were Greek Sea People who settled[97]
The southern Levant and with Phoenicians shared
Iron tools and new ideas, so Israel was nettled
And neither Goliath[98] nor Delilah[99] were spared.

The Nile Delta's a land of opportunities,
Phoenicians at Memphis brought more than passing trade,
They built workshops and shrines, long-lived communities; [100]
At Pi-Rameses, also, deep connections were made.

With Hebrews they sailed south, Aqaba to Ophir
For sandalwood, pearls, gold and to bring India near.[101]
At Pharaoh Necho's word a mighty trip was planned
Down Africa's east coast past Zanzibar, they land,
Grow quick crops, round Good Hope then head home by the west.[102]
A myth maybe but yet, a suitably Phoenician quest.

---

97 There are striking similarities between the last Mycenean pottery and the earliest Philistine ceramics, Amos 9.7 and Jeremiah 47.4 confirm that the Philistines came from Caphtor which is mostly identified with Crete and DNA testing reveals strong links between early Philistines and the Aegean (*National Geographic* 4/7/2019).
98 1 Samuel 17.
99 Judges 16.
100 Herodotus *The Histories* II.112.
101 1 Kings 9: 26-8, 10: 11.
102 Herodotus *The Histories* IV.45.

*Homeland*

**Hebrews**

As fellow Canaanites, Phoenicians and Hebrews
Share common ancestry[103] and many social views,
Jointly sail to Tarshish for metal, tusks and apes,[104]
And Solomon's Temple their united team shapes.

Tyre's princess Jezebel wed Ahab, Hebrew king,[105]
Brought Baal with her to pray, Yahweh's priests feel the sting,
Her eunuchs then conspire, out the window she flies,[106]
And Ezekiel prophesies Tyre's fiery demise.[107]

Yet Moses taught equality before the law[108]
And power to the people's council as their voice.[109]
In Israel judges led and spoke out for the poor,
Selected for their wisdom by the people's choice.
Even with kings they kept alive these traditions
And so had much to teach and influence the Phoenicians.[110]

---

103 M.F. Hammer (2000) 'Jewish and Middle Eastern non-Jewish populations share a common pool of Y-chromosome biallelic haplotypes' *Proceedings of the National Academy of Sciences* 97(12): 6769-74. For a more recent and general account, see Lawler 'DNA from the Bible's Canaanites...' Note 23 above.
104 1 Kings 10:22.
105 1 Kings 16: 31.
106 2 Kings 9: 30-33.
107 Ezekiel 26-28.
108 See for example Deuteronomy 17: 19-20.
109 See Moses's deference to the council at Numbers 14: 4-5.
110 The impact of Hebrew proto-democratic processes on the West is discussed in T.H. Oesterley and W.O.E. Robinson (1932) *History of Israel* Oxford: Clarendon Press Vol II: 105, C.U. Wolf (1947) 'Traces of Primitive Democracy in Ancient Israel' *Journal of Near Eastern Studies* 6(2): 98-108 and Martin Buber (1967) *Kingship of God* New York: Harper & Row. I have previously explored the transmission of these processes through the Phoenician trading routes to ancient Greece in 'Israel and Phoenicia' in B. Isakhan & S. Stockwell (eds) (2012) *The Edinburgh Companion to the History of Democracy* Edinburgh: Edinburgh University Press: 71-81.

*The Phoenician Sonnets*

# Greek Sphere of Influence

*The Phoenician Sonnets*

*Greek Sphere of Influence*

**Kition**

Sail west from Phoenicia, there's Cyprus in a day,
Its jewel is Kition, hub of the copper trade,[111]
Minoans came to buy, Myceneans came to stay,[112]
In time a temple to the great goddess is made.

It falls after earthquake and then insurrection
But Tyre comes to rebuild a shrine to Astarte
Where metal's worked under her detailed direction
And her fertility sought with worship hearty.[113]

Cyprus becomes part of Phoenicia extended,
Artists orientalise, Zeno founds Stoicism,[114]
War comes, Cyprus backs Persia, all is up-ended,
The temple is in peril, Greeks win the schism,
Astarte becomes Aphrodite, love prevails,
The Greek goddess spreads Astarte's strength along western trails.

---

111 Markoe *Phoenicians:* 39
112 Woolmer *A Short History:* 182
113 Among the religious devotions practised at Astarte's temples was 'sacred prostitution' where men and women who had their prayers answered provided sexual services to encourage fertility among the gods and in nature: see Woolmer *A Short History:* 71 and with particular regard to Cyprus, Herodotus *The Histories:* I: 199.
114 Zeno of Kition (c. 334-262 BCE), recognised as the founder of the Stoic school of philosophy, is described as Phoenician by Crates in Diogenes Laertius (c. 230 CE) *The Lives of Eminent Philosophers* Book VII.1.1-3.

*The Phoenician Sonnets*

## Ships

Phoenician ships were famed, made with advanced techniques,
From finest cedar carved, they're strong and sturdy boats.
Their cargo ships, *gauloi,* the safest thing that floats
Round hull, deep draft, it takes large loads and rarely leaks.

Their workhorse was *hippoi,* smaller and more agile,
It's good to nip about harbours along the coast.[115]
Their warships swift and sleek, a terrifying host,
Their bows armed with bronze beaks made other ships fragile.[116]

All ships had painted eyes on each side of the prow
To spread fear among foes and see the way back home.
Despite how well they're built, some sank beneath the foam
And, from their wrecks, lessons can still be learnt right now.
In Marsala Museum an ancient ship survives
Its ordered construction tells much about Phoenician lives.[117]

---

115 Markoe *Phoenicians:* 97.
116 ibid: 80.
117 The salvaged ship in the Baglio Anselmi Archaeological Museum in Marsala, Sicily (visited 2010) is Carthaginian and was most likely sunk in the 241 BCE Battle of the Egadi Islands that ended the First Punic War. It was pre-fabricated and imported to the region in pieces marked with alphabetical letters that only had to be matched for speedy construction.

*The Phoenician Sonnets*

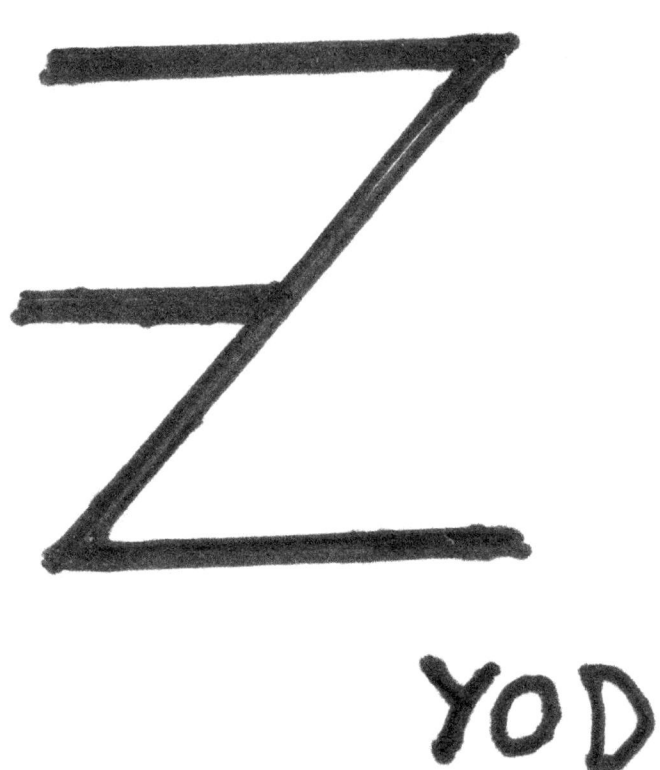

*Greek Sphere of Influence*

## Rhodes

West from Cyprus along the coast now called Turkish
Phoenician traders came to the Greek Isle of Rhodes,
A hub where ships could spend some time and refurbish
While selling fine ivories, charms, shells and jewels in loads.[118]

Some stayed, made workshops there, taught locals how to make
Glittering trinkets and fine plate and things from glass
That still astound – like ground lenses for science's sake,
To peer close at and put things in phylum and class.[119]

Sitting in the old town square insight came to me:
The Phoenician contribution to history,
Was not imperial as was the Greeks' and Romans',
And Mussolini's bent, but brought better omens:
Ideas inquisitive, practical but complex,
To find solutions to conundrums, some that still perplex.

---

118 Markoe *Phoenicians:* 171.
119 In the Rhodes Archaeological Museum (visited 2010) there is a set of plano-convex magnifying glasses made of rock crystal, some set in bronze frames with engravings indicating their different focal lengths. They were found in the Ialysos sanctuary and are dated between the 7th and 6th centuries BCE at the peak of Phoenician influence on Rhodes. They are perhaps the oldest known magnifying glasses in the world and while they were probably used for jewellery work and engraving seals, their application to scientific purposes is apparent.

# The Phoenician Sonnets

## Europa

Tyre's princess Europa was spied by great god Zeus,
She spurned his affections, so he became a bull
So beautiful she fell in love, reason's no use.
He kidnapped her to Crete, their three sons had great pull

As heroes, kings and judges of the underworld.[120]
Zeus left her queen of Crete with jewels and robot guard,
Deft dog, sure spear and Minotaur in labyrinth hurled,[121]
Recalling crafts and schemes at which Phoenicians starred.

Europa's father sent his sons to find the girl,
Cadmus and his keen crew went far without success,
But the alphabet and knowledge they did unfurl,
Killing dragons, founding cities, ending duress.[122]
Cadmus built Thebes, he took Harmonia as his wife,
He never found Europa but he brought Europe to life.[123]

---

120  For dramatic accounts of the Europa story, see Euripides play (410 BCE [1942]) 'Hypsipyle' in D.L. Page (trans) *Greek Literary Papyri* Vol 1 London: Heinemann: 87 and Ovid (8 CE) *Metamorphosis* II.833-III.137. For a more prosaic account consider Herodotus *The Histories:* I.2.
121  In the traditional mythology the Minotaur comes a generation after Europa when her son Minos becomes king of Crete and then step-father of a half-man, half-bull monster who, by the grace of Zeus, is lured into the labyrinth from which he cannot escape.
122  The claim that Cadmus brought the alphabet to Greece is made by Herodotus *The Histories* V.58-61. Even in ancient times the dragons were seen as metaphors for outmoded mythological thinking.
123  Robert S. P. Beekes rejects a Phoenician connection for either Cadmus or Europa in his 2004 'Kadmos and Europa, and the Phoenicians' *Kadmos* 43(1): 167-184 but as mythological rather than historical figures it is not surprising that their stories have been rewritten to reflect actual cultural transmission.

*The Phoenician Sonnets*

*Greek Sphere of Influence*

**The Ionian Coast**

On north from Rhodes to Kos and the Ionian Coast,
Wine jars and perfume flasks mark the Phoenician way[124]
As does the early test of free, frank speech towns host,
A pattern repeated where the Phoenicians stay.

In Samos fine brass works and funeral gifts to gods,[125]
The Chios sphinx, Erythrae's Heracles from Tyre[126]
Show Eastern influence in towns that all gave nods
To democracy before Athens took it higher.[127]

But Miletus is different, while tyrants rule
New, free ideas come forth from Phoenician enclaves,
Informed by travel to Egypt and Babylon,[128]
The nascent scientific method is their tool
So Thales predicts eclipses and crop yields and braves
The wrath of Zeus to teach materialism and pure reason.[129]

---

124 Markoe *Phoenicians:* 171, 173; E. Lipinski (2004) *Itineraria Phoenicia* Leuven: Peeters: 155.
125 R. Osborne (2009) *Greece in the Making, 1200-479BC* London: Routledge: 86-87.
126 Pausanias *Description of Greece* VII.5.5.
127 E.W. Robinson (1997) *The First Democracies* Stuttgart: Franz Steiner Verlag: Kos 103-104; Samos 118-120; Chios 90-101. For Erythrae, see Aristotle (c. 350 BCE) *Politics* 1305b 18-23.
128 Jöran Friberg (2007) *Amazing Traces of a Babylonian Origin in Greek Mathematics* River Edge: World Scientific. On Thales specifically, see B. L. Van der Waerden (1961) *Science Awakening* (trans A. Dresden) New York: Oxford University Press: 5.
129 J. Barnes (2001) *Early Greek Philosophy* (2nd rev. ed.) London: Penguin: 9-17.

*The Phoenician Sonnets*

## Science

Phoenician ways were simple but systematic,
Digging ditches,[130] building bridges,[131] setting up ships,[132]
Their practical approach was prized, their wits were quick:
They learnt maths and astronomy on trading trips.

Philo of Byblos quotes the Beirut sage[133] who wrote,
In times remote, that life evolved from watery slime:
A wet world of matter needing no gods of note,
Ideas that reappear in Greek Hesiod's time.[134]

Pherecydes draws lines between real and divine,
Insights inspired by "secret Phoenician books".[135]
Born from Phoenician kin, Thales says the first thing's brine
And steers humans away from supernatural hooks,[136]
Socrates agrees, the idea hits full throttle
In the materialistic methods of Aristotle.[137]

---

130 Herodotus *The Histories:* VII.23.
131 Herodotus *The Histories:* VII.33-35.
132 Xenophon (c. 360 BCE) *Oeconomicus:* VIII.
133 The sage was Sanchuniathon who is said to have lived before the Trojan War (dated to 1180 BCE), see Baumgarten *The Phoenician History of Philo of Byblos:* 6-7.
134 ibid: 96. Josephine Quinn (2017) *In Search of the Phoenicians* Princeton: Princeton University Press: 146 dates the text to the Hellenistic period (starting 332 BCE) but perhaps the Phoenicians had a materialist approach all along that they transmitted into the Greek sphere around Hesiod's time (700 BCE).
135 West *Early Greek Philosophy and the Orient*: 1-3.
136 Barnes *Early Greek Philosophy:* 9-17.
137 Anna Makolkin (2016) 'Phoenician Cosmology as a Proto-base for Greek Materialism, Naturalist Philosophy and Aristotelianism' *Biocosmology* 6: 3&4.

*The Phoenician Sonnets*

*Greek Sphere of Influence*

## Aegean

Cadmus and his Phoenician crew crossed the Aegean,
On Thasos they turned mountains upside down for gold
And built a temple to Heracles the Tyrian;[138]
Some went to Lemnos with Sidon's famed silver bowl, [139]

They led the way for Jason and his Argonauts,
Past Troy's burnt ruins and Byzantium to the Black Sea,
Trading for amber and fur at the farthest ports
And dabbling in the shameful trade of slavery.[140]

Then south to Euboea with prestige goods and trinkets,
To Naxos and Argos, more trade most politic[141]
And myths prefiguring the gods of Olympus.[142]
I love this wine dark sea, these places historic,
Phoenician objects there show them ready to deal,
That they brought ideas too reflects their intellectual zeal.

---

138 Herodotus *The Histories* VI.47, II.44.
139 Homer *The Iliad* XXIII.749ff: Sidonians give a magnificent bowl to Thoas, king of Lemnos which is used to ransom Lycaon from Patroclus or, ibid XXI.34ff, Achilles. It becomes a prize in the games Achilles holds to commemorate Patroclus.
140 Woolmer *A Short History* 66; Jan Bouzek (2018) *Studies of Homeric Greece* Prague: Karolinum: 173-174 offers a summary of evidence of Phoenician activity around the Black Sea; Ezekiel 27: 13 says 'Greece, Tubal and Meshek did business with you; they traded human beings… for your wares.' Josephus (c. 97 CE *Antiquities of the Jews* I.6.1) claims Tubal was Georgia and Sir Walter Raleigh (1614 CE *History of the World* I.8.6) spreads the idea Meshek was Moscow though modern scholars are inclined to see them as Anatolian tribes.
141 For trade with these places, see Markoe *Phoenicians:* 173-174. As locales of early popular government, see Robinson *The First Democracies*: Chalcis on Euboea 88-90; Naxos 117-118; Argos 82-88.
142 J.L. Weston (1920) *From Ritual to Romance* Cambridge: Cambridge University Press touches on the transmission of gods and mythology from east to west but M.L. West (1997) *The East Face of Helicon: West Asiatic Elements in Greek Poetry and Myth* Oxford: Clarendon Press addresses the question in a broad and systematic fashion.

## The Phoenician Sonnets

Author adresses
Athanian Pnyx,
home of democracy

*Greek Sphere of Influence*

**Democracy**

Greeks gave democracy form, content and a name
But did it spring unbidden from the Attic soil
Or did it start early in the human time frame
When speech let First Nations put debate on the boil?[143]

There're democratic forms found in our first cities:
In ancient India, China and old Iraq,[144]
It's primitive but boosts social affinities
That flourish in Phoenicia when royal regimes crack.

Arwad, Byblos, Sidon, Irqata, Tunip, Tyre,
All try popular rule or councils over kings.
Did the idea go west and ancient Greeks inspire?
Like alphabet and science, democracy springs
At locales along the Phoenician trading route
Where cultural intercourse came to bear political fruit.[145]

---

143 P. Watson and B. Barber (1990) *The Struggle for Democracy* London: Allen & Co: 55-85 traces the origins of Greek democracy to the processes of tribal consultation. Kenneth Maddock (1974) *The Australian Aborigines* Ringwood: Penguin: 166 points out that these consultations were typically governed by the principle of "egalitarian mutuality" that remains at the heart of best democratic practice today. See also Immaculate Kizza (2011) 'Africa's Indigenous Democracies' and Larissa Behrendt (2011) 'Aboriginal Democracy and Australia' in B. Isakhan & S. Stockwell (eds) *The Secret History of Democracy* London: Palgrave MacMillan: 123-135; 148-161.

144 Steven Muhlberger (2011) 'Republics and Quasi-Democratic Institutions in Ancient India'; Pauline Keating (2011) 'Digging for Democracy in China'; and Ben Isakhan (2011) 'What's so 'Primitive about "Primitive Democracy"?' in Isakhan & Stockwell *The Secret History of Democracy*: 49-59; 60-75; 19-34; also Thorkild Jacobsen (1970 [1943]) 'Primitive Democracy in Ancient Mesopotamia' in W.L. Moran (ed), *Toward the Image of Tammuz* Massachusetts: Harvard University Press: 157-170.

145 Eric Robinson's *The First Democracies* notes twenty city-states with various experience of popular free rule before 508 BCE when Kleisthenes' reforms introduced mature democracy to Athens. By my account four-fifths of those were on or adjacent to the Phoenician trading route, see S. Stockwell (2011) 'Before Athens' Isakhan & Stockwell *The Secret History of Democracy*: 35-48.

*The Phoenician Sonnets*

MEM

## Athens

First a tribe on a rock a long way from the sea,
Athens' trade in silver and slaves saw it enlarge,
Into a centre of art and philosophy:
Cultural politicking let it take charge.

A long walk from its port, Phoenicians rarely came,
But their letters and art were most influential[146]
And when social turmoil became more than a game
Democracy became an idea essential.

Critics are sceptical re transfer to Athens,
Just how was the Phoenician seed transplanted there?[147]
Herodotus already knew – the assassins
Harmodius and Aristogiton – the pair
Were from a Cadmean clan, steeped in equality,
They struck the tyrant down and that brought on democracy.[148]

---

146 There is evidence of Phoenician contact with Athens from the 9th century BCE in gold work including granulation and filigree that 'must have been learnt from the east' as well 'a Phoenician bronze bowl, faience disks and ivory seals' Osborne *Greece in the Making*: 62, 158.
147 Kurt Raaflaub (2005) 'Poets, lawgivers, and the beginnings of political reflection in archaic Greece' in C. Rowe & M. Schofield *The Cambridge History of Greek and Roman Political Thought* Cambridge: Cambridge University Press: 52.
148 Herodotus *The Histories*: V: 55-7. Harmodius and Aristogiton are celebrated for bringing freedom and equality to Athens and as foundational to democracy in a drinking song collected by Athenaeus of Naucratis (200 CE [1854]) *The Deipnosophists or Banquet of the Learned* (trans C.D. Yonge) London: Bohn: XV.50.x-xiii.

*The Phoenician Sonnets*

Wild Goat Jug
Miletos 6ᵀᴴ C BCE

*Greek Sphere of Influence*

**Orientalising Art**

After the Minoans' time art was geometric,
Phoenicians gave a gift, brought action figures back.
We see their craft in Crete, with design kinetic –
A diadem of heroes fighting lion attack –

Starts a new school of fine, figured metalworking
That makes the stunning shields found in Mt Ida's shrine.[149]
In Athens too their bowl, bronze images lurking[150]
Precedes style seen adorning Parthenon's fine line.[151]

Oriental art spreads up the Ionian coast:
From eastern ivory trees of life with goats, threads lead
To pots in wild goat style which keep buyers engrossed
With exquisite detail that fills a psychic need –[152]
There's a naturalism that helps stories be told,
Then sphinxes and gryphons come, it's mythological gold.[153]

---

149 J.N. Coldstream (1982) 'Greeks and Phoenicians in the Aegean' in H.G. Niemeyer (ed) *Phonizier in Westen* Mainz: Zaben: 268.
150 Markoe *Phoenician Bowls:* 201-202.
151 The Elgin Marbles presently in the British Museum, visited 2016.
152 As seen in Rhodes Archaeological Museum, visited 2010.
153 Walter Burkert (1992) *The Orientalizing Revolution: Near Eastern influence on Greek culture in the early archaic age* Cambridge, Mass: Harvard University Press.

*The Phoenician Sonnets*

*Greek Sphere of Influence*

## Crete

Hard west from Phoenicia is the island of Crete,
Grave goods, a shrine and mines speak of long connections.[154]
At first we meet Minoans, adventurers complete
Jumping bulls, juggling snakes, poppy introspections,[155]

They traded far and wide, there's many eastern link.[156]
Earthquakes and revolt saw Mycenaeans take their place,
But when their palaces fell, Phoenicians barely blink,
Bring art, faience and wine as westwards their ships trace.

Enclaves of Phoenicians flourish around Knossos,
Fine craft and detailed art prompt locals to engage.[157]
Traders go south to the cosmic coast near Kommos,
There are rich mines of iron, the metal of the age,
To praise the gods they built a tri-pillared temple[158]
That even now calls up forces strange and elemental.

---

154 Markoe *Phoenicians:* 172-173.
155 See Heraklion Archaeological Museum, visited 2002.
156 Stylianos Alexiou (n.d.) *Minoan Civilization* Heraklion: Kouvidis-Manouras Co. For connections to the East, see pages 9, 39, 71, 132-3; also Anon. (1936) 'Minoan Influences in Ancient Syria' *Nature* 138: 357.
157 Osborne *Greece in the Making:* 63-64.
158 Joseph W. Shaw (1989) 'Phoenicians in Southern Crete' *American Journal of Archaeology* 93: 165-183.

*The Phoenician Sonnets*

*Greek Sphere of Influence*

## Homer

Homer is a mystery, was he one man or two?
Or was he many voices chiming down through time?
Or blind and far-sighted, oral and literate too?[159]
We're left with two great tales and poesy in its prime.

The *Iliad* sees Phoenicians praised for their craft,
So Hecuba's best gown is stitched by Sidon girls[160]
And brave Achilles' prize for he who runs most fast
Is Sidon's 'rich, wrought' bowl with decorative twirls.[161]

The later *Odyssey* claims craft's from deity,[162]
Phoenicians are portrayed as thieves and kidnappers[163]
Who plot to sell Ulysses into slavery.[164]
They're billed as mad, bad guys 'cause trade war now matters.
Yet while the Greeks and Phoenicians bicker and feud
It's by the latter's routes Ulysses comes home to his brood.[165]

---

159 Emily Wilson gives a detailed account of the history of, and recent responses to, the Homeric question in the introduction to her 2018 translation of *The Odyssey* New York: Norton: 5-13.
160 Homer *The Iliad* VI.288ff.
161 ibid XXIII.740ff.
162 For example, Hephaestus, god of smiths and craft, is credited with the finely crafted silver bowl the king of Sidon gives to Menelaus: Homer *The Odyssey* IV.613-619, again XV.114-116.
163 As the swineherd Eumaeus tells his master, Ulysses, in his story of how he became a slave: ibid XV.414-481.
164 As Ulysses claims in his tall tale to Eumaeus: ibid XIV.288-297.
165 In the tall tale Ulysses tells Athena, Phoenicians bring him from Crete to Ithaca before returning to Sidon: ibid XIII.273-286. Attempts to reconstruct Ulysses' wanderings point to a westerly arc to Tunisia, Sicily, Sardinia, the Balearics and Spain, all along Phoenician trading routes. Also Menelaus follows what sounds like a Phoenician itinerary on his way home: Cyprus, Phoenicia, Egypt, Ethiopia, Sidon, Arabia and Libya ibid IV.81-84.

*The Phoenician Sonnets*

## Peloponnese

Surprisingly Sparta had some Phoenician links –[166]
Though inland quite a way there's purple at its port,[167]
Mad masks and ivory gifts at the holy hi-jinks[168]
Have Punic tastes as does their political thought:

Both Sparta and Carthage have two equal leaders
Watched over by a careful council of their peers,
A democratic form resting on good speakers,
A balance of power, few tyrannical fears.[169]

There's Phoenician traces 'round the Peloponnese:
Kythera has purple works and Astarte's shrine;[170]
Ithaka's where Phoenicians dropped home Ulysses;[171]
Olympia's bronze and Heracles take eastern lines.[172]
Past Elis and Achaea, o'er the Adriatic
The route takes us to Italy and changes dramatic.

---

166 Herodotus *The Histories* IV.147-149 tracks the Phoenician heritage of the Aegidae, a powerful Spartan clan.
167 Sparta's port was Gytheion, see Markoe *Phoenicians:* 173.
168 The sanctuary of Artemis Orthia on Sparta's outskirts was the site of rambunctious religious celebrations and votive offerings recovered from the area include Phoenician influenced masks and ivories, see W. Culican (1975) 'Some Phoenician Masks and Other Terracottas' *Berytus Archaeological Studies* 24: 55-64.
169 Aristotle was an early commentator who pointed out the similarities between the Spartan and Carthaginian constitutions, see his *Politics:* 1273a.
170 Markoe *Phoenicians:* 172-173.
171 According to the tall tale he tells Athena: Homer *The Odyssey* XIII.273-282.
172 Re bronze, see Phoenician bowls in Olympia Archaeological Museum and National Archaeological Museum, Athens (both visited 2010) and Elanor Guralnick (2004) 'A Group of Eastern Bronzes from Olympia' *American Journal of Archaeology* 108: 2: 187-222; re the statue of Heracles originally from Tyre, see Pausanias *Description of Greece* V.25.12.

*The Phoenician Sonnets*

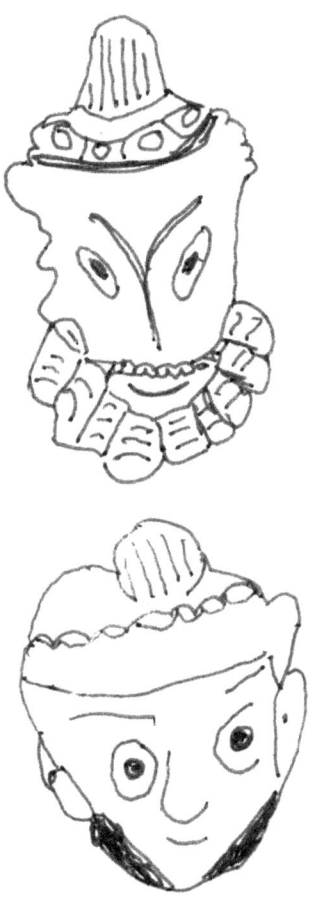

Faience Heads
Bardo Museum
Carthage

*Greek Sphere of Influence*

## Trade… and Slaves

Ezekiel catalogues the trade Phoenicia spreads:[173]
Cypress, cedar and oak, metals both raw and wrought
Blood purple dye, sweet cane, wheat grain and faience heads,
Lambs, rams and goats, their wool, steeds, mules and spice reached port.

Coral, rubies, turquoise, ivory and ebony,
Gold, rugs and wine, oils, balms and tusks, embroidered clothes.
Phoenicians trade across language groups quite fairly,
Barter with local folk, accept what they propose.[174]

But slaves. Here's contradiction, freedom loving folk
Respect others yet profit from human traffic.
Democracy had a fatal flaw, the slave's yoke
Is what bought citizens time for culture classic.[175]
Slavery's still a problem that has not gone away,
It's all around us in disguise, we must fight it today.

---

173 Ezekiel 27.
174 For more on 'dumb barter' techniques, see Herodotus *The Histories* IV.196.
175 Paulin Ismard (2017) *Democracy's Slaves: A Political History of Ancient Greece* Cambridge, Mass: Harvard University Press.

*The Phoenician Sonnets*

*Greek Sphere of Influence*

## To Sicily

The trade route first followed Italy's southern shore,
In Sybaris we see a Phoenician bronze bowl
With animals and gods from before Greeks made war[176]
And pushed the trade route south, making Malta the goal.

Then west to Sicily where Phoenicians start trade
'All round'[177] as pots and scarabs from Syracuse show.[178]
The Greeks settled the east, so Carthage strongholds made
At western ports like Soluntum and Palermo.

Motya, most western isle, secure in its lagoon,[179]
Made trade with local folk and big fleets passing by,
Brought temples, art and wealth and city walls quite soon.
Then Greeks built a causeway, let their catapults fly
And burnt that bright town down.[180] As dusk falls on the ruins,
We feel history flow fast and how short life is for humans.

---

176 National Archaeological Museum of Sibaritide (visited 2010).
177 Thucydides *The History of the Peloponnesian War* XVIII.2.
178 Markoe *Phoenician Bowls*: 145.
179 A succinct account of Motya's geography and history is provided by Aldo Volpi and M.P. Toti (2007) *Motya* Marsala: La Medusa Editrice. Whitaker Museum, Motya (visited 2010).
180 In 397 BCE, see Diodorus Siculus (c. 50 BCE) *Library of History:* XIV.47-52.

# The Phoenician Sonnets

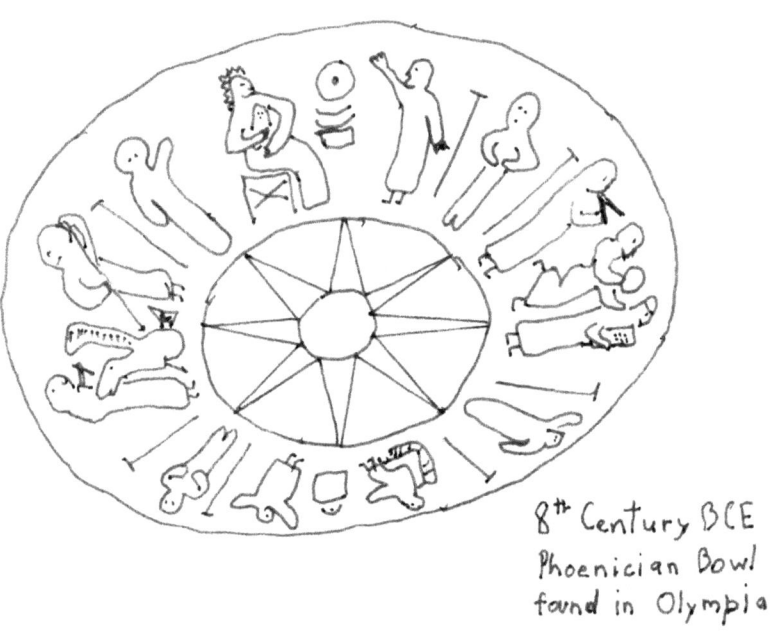

8th Century BCE
Phoenician Bowl
found in Olympia

## Bowls

First found in Tuscany, then Cyprus, Nimrud, Greece,
The bowls, embossed, incised, are silver, bronze or gold,
Their purpose is prestige in life then when deceased,
The bowl's own odyssey gives fame forever told.

They have Egyptian gods and strong Assyrian kings,
There's battles, beasts and hunting scenes, gryphons and sphinx
Circling floral medallions in orderly rings,
There's many cultures here and many story links.[181]

They're called Phoenician bowls but is that really right?
For none have yet been found in a true homeland site.
Perhaps travelling tradesmen made them for local kings
Or far-flung workshops served those searching for bling things
But context where they're found, with ivory, jewels and pots,
Mark them as Phoenician whatever their production spots.

---

181 Markoe *Phoenician Bowls* remains a comprehensive summary of what we know about Phoenician bowls. For a recent update touching on new finds and debates around the bowls: Nicholas Vella (2010) '"Phoenician" Metal Bowls: Boundary Objects in the Archaic Period' *Bollettino di Archeologia* Volume speciale A:A2:5.

# The Phoenician Sonnets

# Carthage and West

*The Phoenician Sonnets*

PE

## Carthage

Queen Dido built Carthage, escaping Tyre's ill-will,[182]
She bought, from locals, land beneath an oxen hide
Then cut the skin into thin strips and girt a hill:
A thriving town grew there with trade and craft inspired.

Carthage was well-designed: strong walls, two ports, wide streets,
Temples to Baal and Bes, a Tophet sanctuary.
There are two chosen leaders plus the people meets
To steer the city's path, like a democracy.[183]

The city's influence spread along Africa's coasts
From Leptis Magna to Mogador and beyond.
Their colonies replace Phoenician trading posts,
The Western Mediterranean became their pond.
But Rome was growing too which prompts three Punic Wars
That only end when Rome destroys Carthage to settle scores.[184]

---

182 The traditional foundation date of Carthage is 814 BCE which now is not far from the archaeological evidence. In some foundation myths Dido is known as Elissa. Richard Miles does useful work disentangling myths and reading them against the archaeology and politics in his (2010) *Carthage Must Be Destroyed* London: Penguin: 58-68; 365-370.
183 For a comprehensive account of the history and political institutions of Carthage, see M.H. Fantar (2007) *Carthage* Tunisia: Alif.
184 First Punic War 264-241 BCE; Second Punic War 219-201 BCE; Third Punic War 149-146 BCE. For an eyewitness account of Carthage's destruction, see Polybius (140 BCE) *The Histories* XXXIX.2-5.

*The Phoenician Sonnets*

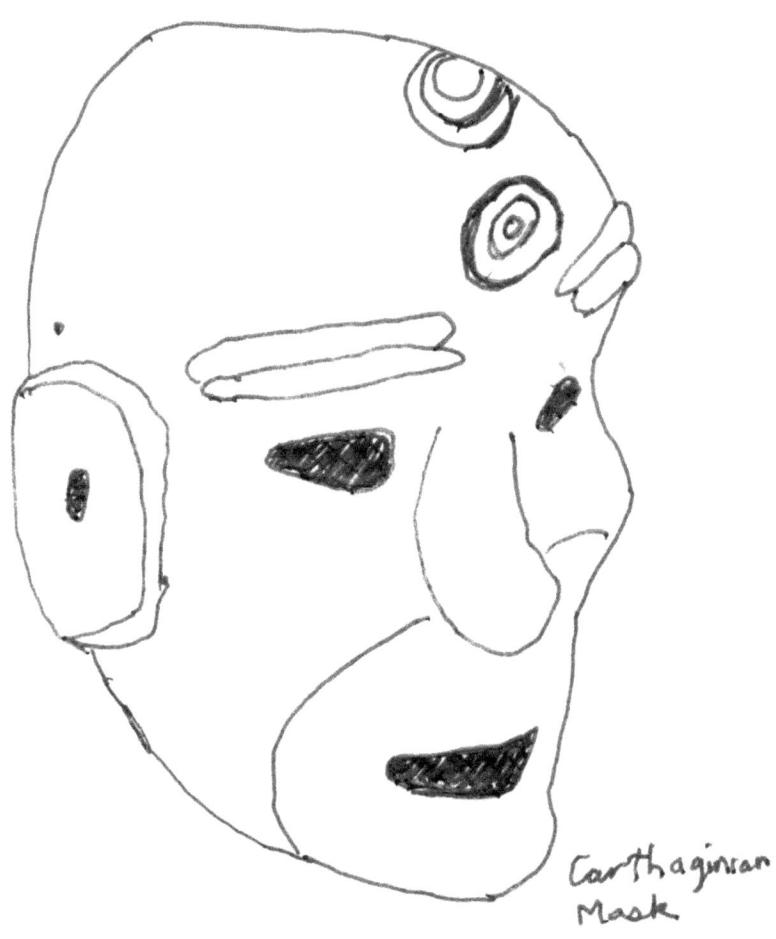

## Hannibal

Hannibal led the elephants over the Alps
And took Carthage's war up to the walls of Rome,
The strategy and speed learnt from Heracles helps[185]
He was the Barca's heir, the war camp was his home.

In Spain he'd trained a loyal and well-oiled fighting corps,
That trashed Rome's legions at Trebia and Trasimene,
His pincer move at Cannae almost won the war,
He controls Italy but is far from serene.

For fifteen long years Rome refuses to surrender,
Worn down Hannibal retreats to rescue Carthage.
Rome herds his elephants back to him at Zama
And though the war is lost, folks still give him homage.[186]
He fights Rome in the East until they track him down,
He kills himself to thwart arrest but always keeps renown.

---

[185] Hannibal's identification with Heracles is detailed in Miles *Carthage Must Be Destroyed:* 245-255. Miles also gives a succinct account of Hannibal's Italian campaign on pages 256-323.
[186] The people of Carthage elected him *suffete*, or co-leader, in 196 BCE.

*The Phoenician Sonnets*

## Sardinia

Metal's the magnet that brought the Phoenicians west,[187]
In Sardinia they mined copper, silver and iron,
Some for trade, some shipped back at Assyria's behest.
The locals marry in, learn eastern fine design.

In the museum we're surprised by the Nora Stone,
It's lurking in shadows but speaks to us 'cross time:
The cost of war, 'Futility', dying men moan,
How better's peace and love with friendship most sublime.[188]

Trading posts turn to towns, each a little different,[189]
Caligari, Nora, Sulky 'n' Tharros grow large,
Mines plus plantations build temples magnificent,
There's tragic tophets too while Carthage is in charge.
After the Second Punic War Rome takes the isle
And in the ruins we see the end to quirky eastern style.

---

187 Markoe *Phoenicians*: 176-179.
188 Dated to c. 800 BCE, the Nora Stone is a war memorial with early Phoenician script. It is in the National Archaeological Museum, Caligari (visited 2014) and its translation is still a matter of debate: celebration of conquest or commemoration of lost comrades? See: F. M. Cross (1972) 'An Interpretation of the Nora Stone' *Bulletin of the American Schools of Oriental Research* 208: 13-19; Nathan Pilkington (2012) 'A Note on Nora and the Nora Stone' *BASOR* 385: 45-51.
189 Andrea Roppa (2014) 'Identifying Punic Sardinia' in J. Quinn & N. Vella *The Punic Mediterranean* Cambridge: Cambridge University Press: 257-281.

*The Phoenician Sonnets*

Sign of Tanit
Carthage Tophet

## Tophets

Around some Punic towns the tophets are still sad,
They're graveyards for children but just how did they die?
The Bible and Romans say sacrifice, that's bad[190]
But is this propaganda, the old-time big lie?

Kid killing's a thing: see Abraham and Isaac,[191]
Greek Agamemnon killed his daughter for good wind,[192]
The Parthenon frieze may tell of a like attack[193]
And Romans drowned hermaphroditic wunderkind.[194]

Forensic evidence of sacrifice is slim,
Most physical remains don't match the known sources,
Miscarriage and infant mortality are grim,
Mostly these children died of natural causes.[195]
And when inscriptions say the children were a gift
Perhaps it means that in their time they gave all lives a lift.[196]

---

190 2 Chronicles 28:3, 33:6; Jeremiah 7:31, 19:2–6; Diodorus Siculus *Library of History* XX.14.
191 Genesis 22.
192 Euripides (c. 407 BCE) *Iphigenia in Aulis*.
193 For the sad story behind the Elgin Marbles, a central feature of the classical heritage, see Joan Breton Connelly (2014) *The Parthenon Enigma*. New York: Knopf. Erechtheus, the mythical king of Athens must sacrifice his daughter to save the city. Connelly argues the frieze's final scene depicts Erechtheus handing his daughter the dress she will wear when she is sacrificed.
194 Celia Schultz (2010) 'The Romans and ritual murder' *Journal of American Academy of Religion* 78(2): 516-541.
195 Jeffrey H. Schwartz (2016) "The Mythology of Carthaginian Child Sacrifice: A Physical Anthropological Perspective" in Carrie Ann Murray (ed), *Diversity of Sacrifice: Form and Function of Sacrificial Practices in the Ancient World and Beyond*. New York: SUNY Press: 103-126.
196 Thanks very much to Jose Angel Zamora Lopez, Instituto de Lenguas y Culturas del Mediterráneo y Oriente Próximo, CCHS, Madrid for his dispassionate analysis of tophet issues that he shared with me in a personal interview in 2014.

*The Phoenician Sonnets*

QOP

## Carthage and West

### Tyrrhenian Sea

In Naples Bay the isle of Ischia sits proud,
At Pithecusae Port, Phoenicians and Greeks share,
From the ninth century, a community there,
They trade fine crafts and feast with locals long and loud.[197]

Up north Etruscans swap metal for eastern skill
That in Arezzo's Chimera we see refined.
Phoenicians and Etruscans build Astarte's shrine,
As Pygri's bilingual gold plates tell and still thrill.[198]

The Battle of Alalia saw them in unity[199]
Defeat the Greeks and open trade upon the sea
As far as Marseilles where the carved tariff suggests
A temple to Baal was built and welcomed all guests.[200]
We met an artist there who told us of his dream
Of travel, trade and mystery, Phoenician eyes agleam.

---

[197] Osborne *Greece in the Making:* 107-110. Archaeological Museum of Pithecusae, Villa Arbusto, Ischia (visited 2019) provides a rare glimpse of the everyday reality of Greek-Phoenician interaction.
[198] S. Moscati (1988) 'The Carthaginian Empire' in Moscati *The Phoenicians:* 54-56. Originals in National Etruscan Museum, Villa Giulia, Rome (visited 2014).
[199] Dated to 535 BCE, see Herodotus *The Histories* I.166-167.
[200] The tariff outlined the fees for sacrificial priests and while the stone has been identified as Carthaginian it is argued that the priests plied their trade at a Marseille temple. See Nathan Pilkington (2019) *The Carthaginian Empire: 550–202 BCE* Lanham: Lexington: 161-162.

*The Phoenician Sonnets*

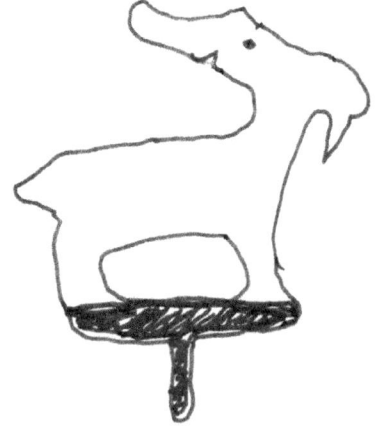

Goat Figurines

*Carthage and West*

**Food**

The Romans saved one thing from Carthage's fiery flames:
Wise Mago's guide to farming grains, meat, vines and fruits.[201]
Phoenician tastes linger along their trading routes:
Grapes, olives, plums and chooks they took as far as Spain.[202]

Beirut: minced beans and meat stuffed with strong local cheese,[203]
Cyprus: beef baked all day with honey, sage and pear,[204]
Rhodes: tender octopus and citrus sauce with care,[205]
Naxos: beetroot, boiled goat and artichokes with peas.[206]

Sicily: white wine, dried tuna roe salted right,[207]
And crumbed fried fish in citrus sauce with spicy bite,[208]
Carthage: fish baked in salt, sweet squid with charcoal tang,[209]
A roadside stall: barbequed lamb with sauce that sang.[210]
In Malaga, grilled sardines on the beach give pause,
We look across the sea and have sardines for second course.

---

201 Miles *Carthage Must Be Destroyed:* 91.
202 F. Hernandez Carrasquilla (1992) 'Some comments on the introduction of domestic fowl in Iberia', *Archaeofauna* 1: 45-53. "Chooks" is an Australian term for domestic fowl.
203 Manara Palace Café, Beirut (these restaurants were visited in 2010).
204 Ithaki Garden, Larnaca, Cyprus.
205 Romiros, Rhodes.
206 Το Ελληνικ□, 'The Greek', Naxos.
207 La Finestra sul Sale, near Motya.
208 Trattoria Pizzeria Zsa, Syracuse.
209 Residence Carthage.
210 On the Nabeul-Tunis road, the sauce was barbequed green peppers, chillies, tomatoes and aubergines blended with olives and oil.

*The Phoenician Sonnets*

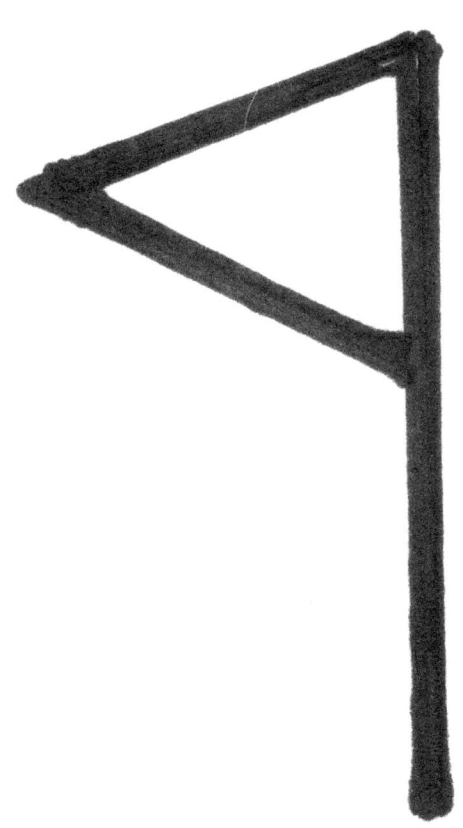

RES

*Carthage and West*

## To the Pillars of Heracles

South down the coast of Spain, by Ibiza's balsam trees
Silver is mined and metal worked for onward trade.
Up Ebro River then down to New Carthage sees
Bulwark of the Barca, home to Hannibal's blade.[211]

Along the Andalusian coast many towns thrive,
Adra, Sexi, Toscanos, Malaga, Cerro.
The African coast too sees many towns alive,
Utica to Rachgoun through Augustine's Hippo.[212]

These routes soon meet at the Pillars of Heracles,
Rock of Gibraltar north and Jebel Musa south,
The end of the old world, the start of a new breeze,
With monsters, trade and dreams past the Atlantic's mouth.
We're surprised in Sexi's Seven Palace's Caves:
Egyptian alabaster vases from Phoenician graves.[213]

---

211 The falcata or machaera Hispania (Seneca c. 59 CE *De Beneficiis* V.24) was made of superior steel (Diodorus Siculus *Library of History* V.33.4).
212 St Augustine of Hippo (354-430 CE), a father of the Catholic Church and author of *The City of God*, identified as Punic: M. Ellingsen (2005) *The Richness of Augustine* Westminster: John Knox Press: 10.
213 These jars were in the Cave of the Seven Palaces, Sexi, now called Alumenacar (visited 2014). They probably contained wine and may have arrived as diplomatic gifts to guarantee the regular delivery of metal ores and food to Egypt (A. Mederos Martín and L.A. Ruiz Cabrero (2002) 'La Fundación De Sexi-Laurita *SPAL* 11: 41-67) or perhaps they came, as is suggested by 'fake' hieroglyphic writing on one of the vases, via the Phoenician homeland as prestige goods for the upper class (M. Pellicer Catalán (2007) *La Necrópolis Laurita (Almuñecar, Granada) En El Contexto De La Colonización Fenicia* Barcelona: Edicions Bellaterra: 54).

*The Phoenician Sonnets*

Heracles in Lionshead Jar

*Carthage and West*

## Heracles

Tyre's Baal, Melqart, to Greeks was half-god Heracles,[214]
Raised in Cadmean Thebes, the gods he scandalised,
Twelve tasks he's set to bring order by strategies:[215]
Strangle the thick-skinned lion,[216] snake's chopped necks cauterised,[217]

Catch fast deer while it sleeps,[218] trap wild boar in deep snow,[219]
Move streams so stables clean,[220] stir bad birds, shoot in flight,[221]
Sneak up and strangle bull,[222] feed wild mares meat to slow[223]
Get queen's belt by asking,[224] steal cows with well-placed might,[225]

Nabs golden apples while giant Atlas holds the skies,[226]
Then learns dark mysteries to bring death's dog from hell.[227]
This trail of tasks – he starts in Greece and Crete then flies
West through his Pillars to Cadiz and Lixus – tell
Of the Phoenician way, as do his logic twists,
By achieving ends in unexpected ways – he persists.

---

214 Markoe *Phoenicians:* 124.
215 Diodorus Siculus *Library of History:* IV.9-39.
216 Kill the Nemean Lion – its impervious skin, removed by its own claws became Heracles cloak.
217 Kill the Hydra of Lerna.
218 Capture the Keryneian Hind.
219 Capture the Erymanthian Boar.
220 Clean the Augean Stables.
221 Disperse the Stymphalian Birds.
222 Capture the Cretan Bull.
223 Rustle the Horses of Diomedes.
224 Steal the Belt of Hippolyte, queen of the Amazons who lived on the Black Sea.
225 Rustle the Cattle of Geryon from west of the pillars of Heracles.
226 Steal the Apples of the Hesperides, a garden near the Atlas Mountains in Morocco.
227 Capture Cerebos, the guard dog of Hades after learning the Eleusinian mysteries.

*The Phoenician Sonnets*

## Cadiz

Phoenicians built Cadiz three millennia ago,
Brought ivory, gold and ostrich eggs from Africa,
Silver ingots from Huelva and Rio Tinto[228]
And tuna, sauce and dried, from the Atlantic far.[229]

They helped local Tartessians' oriental phase,
Taught them the alphabet and put them in the know
Re wine, the potters' wheel and metal-working ways
As seen best in the treasure of Carambolo.[230]

Under the Puppet Theatre in old Cadiz town,
We saw the daily life the residents pursued,
Paved streets, terrace houses with kitchens where grain's ground
Bread's baked and food's preserved while dinner dishes stewed.
They made cowrie earrings and salted fish in vats,
All carefully perused by ever-present hungry cats.[231]

---

228 Markoe *Phoenicians:* 182-184.
229 Strabo *The Geography* (III.2.7) writes enthusiastically about the plump and plentiful tuna available in the area.
230 Sebastian Celestino and Carolina Lopez-Ruiz (2016) *Tartessos and the Phoenicians in Iberia* Oxford: Oxford University Press.
231 Puppet Theatre Archaeological Site, Cadiz (visited 2014). J.A. Zamora López et al (2010) 'Epígrafes fenicios arcaicos en la excavación del Teatro Cómico de Cádiz (2006-2010)' *Rivista di Studi Fenici*, 38(2): 203-236.

*The Phoenician Sonnets*

Bronze Horse Bit Astarte

## Mining

Mining and metal trade were the Phoenicians' quest
From Cyprus to Sardinia and on to Spain.[232]
While locals dug it up, Phoenicians smelt the best,
Made ingots, weapons, jewels, bowls decorative and plain.

Iron, copper, lead and tin, gold, silver, bronze and zinc
To work them well you need the mix and heat exact,
The science of the smith is harder than you think,
They spread their skills afar, deep thought comes with the pact.[233]

Their workmanship was of the highest quality,
The pieces are quite light yet glow and sparkle bright.
Tracing, chasing, granulation and filigree,
Etching and repoussé, many techniques joined tight[234]
To catch the eye and tell a tale or just inspire,
The treasures of the earth were wrought to set the mind afire.

---

232 Markoe *Phoenicians:* 95.
233 The breadth and complexity of Phoenician metalworking is apparent from archaeological finds in Huelva, see F. Gonzalez de Canales et al (2006) 'The Pre-colonial Phoenician Emporium of Huelva ca 900-770 BC' *BABesch* 81: 22-24.
234 For details of Phoenician metal-working and jewellery-making, see Markoe *Phoenicians:* 148-153.

*The Phoenician Sonnets*

*Carthage and West*

## Morocco

The trading post Tingis became the town Tangier,
Its monumental tombs[235] and rock-cut graves speak clear
Phoenician influence[236] and guard the trade route south
To Lixus where metals moved from the river mouth.[237]

There ancient finds attest long contact with the east[238]
Where Heracles tricked Atlas for Hesperides' feast.[239]
South to Chellah, a Punic post with its own coins[240]
While inland Volubis the alphabet purloins.[241]

On south the fabled 'purple isle' of Mogador
Where murex snared 'in weighted and baited baskets',[242]
Are shipped with tusks and ostrich eggs to rich markets[243]
Far from where trade routes end at this seasonal store.
Here sailors left their names, now found on broken plates,[244]
Like them we watch the sun set fast and consider our fates.

---

235 W. Culican (1991) 'Phoenicia and Phoenician Colonization' in J. Boardman et al (eds) *The Assyrian and Babylonian Empires and Other States of the Near East, 8th to 6th Centuries B.C.*, The Cambridge Ancient History, 2nd ed, Vol III/2 Cambridge: Cambridge University Press: 540.
236 Eleftheria Pappa (2009) 'Reflections on the Earliest Phoenician Presence in North-West Africa' *Talanta* XL-XLI: 53-72.
237 Markoe *Phoenicians:* 188.
238 Pliny *The Natural History:* XIX.63 dates the Lixus to 1180 BCE but the oldest remnants found there are 8th century BCE (Carmen Aranegui et al 2011 'The Strait and Beyond: Local Communities in Phoenician Lixus' in Claudia Sagona (ed) *Ceramics of the Phoenician-Punic World* Leuven: Peeters: 297-326.)
239 Pliny *The Natural History* XIX.22.
240 M.H. Fantar (1988) 'North Africa' in Moscati *The Phoenicians:* 180.
241 At the Volubilis and Rabat Museums and the Musee de Kasbah in Tangiers (visited 2014) there are steles from Volubis inscribed with a local alphabet that has some Phoenician characteristics but its own distinctive 'Libyan' style.
242 Winchester *Atlantic:* 67-68.
243 Markoe *Phoenicians:* 188.
244 As seen in the National Archaeology Museum in Rabat as well as the Sidi Mohammed ben Abdallah Museum at Essaouira near Mogador (visited 2014).

*The Phoenician Sonnets*

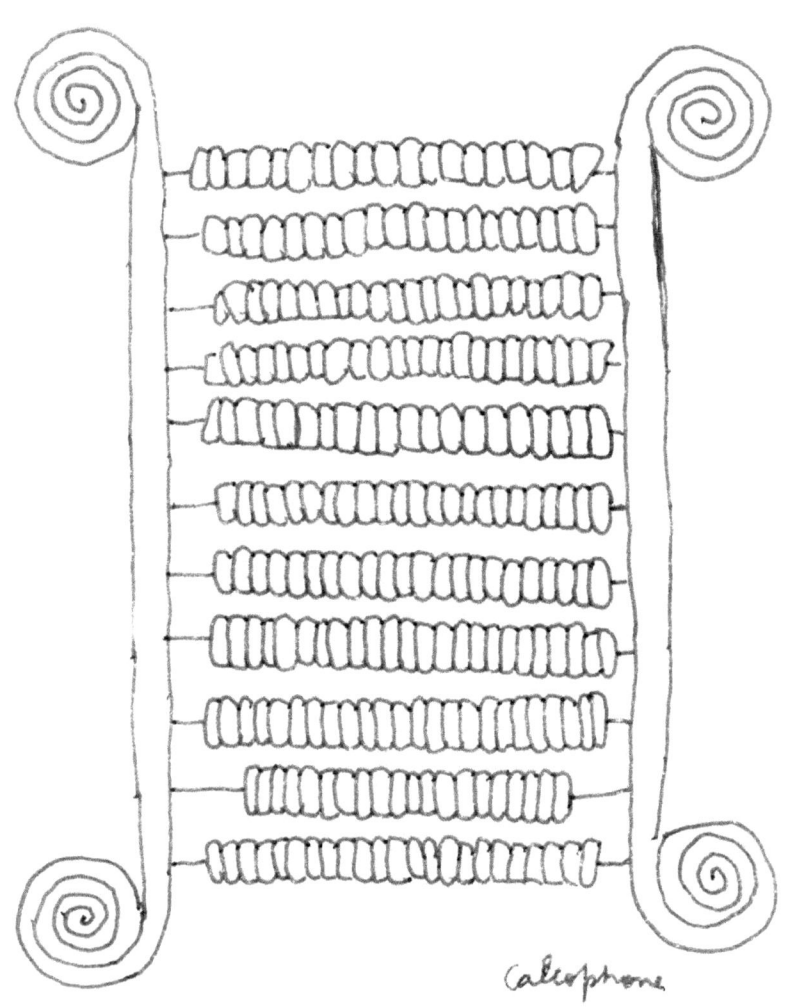

## Music

In Ugarit they found the first musical score[245]
A song for sweet Nikkal, the goddess of ripe fruit,
The lilting lyre and drums assist the voice to soar,
A hymn to creation - syncopation astute.

One Nimrud ivory shows Phoenicians playing pipes
With tambourines and calcophones for Astarte,[246]
Other ivories catch girls in dance of many types
And Carthage rang to bells and cymbals most holy.[247]

The prophet said: 'Thy songs will cease; thy harps fall quiet'[248]
but on the trading route their music still has bite:
In Fez we find the Sacred Music Festival,
Phoenician beats lift hearts, as Maltese drummers tell;[249]
In Carthage 'twas hip-hop helped people fight their fears[250]
While Pythagoras danced on, singing the music of his spheres.[251]

---

245 Haydar *Ugarit:* 26-7.
246 British Museum N 969. The calcophone (sometimes chalcophone) is a musical instrument made of two vertical bars with spiralled terminals as resonators and with eleven bronze springs coiled around connecting pins, played like a cymbal.
247 Mireia López-Bertranand and Agnès Garcia-Ventura (2008) 'Materializing Music and Sound in Some Phoenician and Punic Contexts' *SAGVNTVM* (P.L.A.V.) 40: 27-36.
248 Ezekiel 26:13.
249 Claudia Sagona (2018) 'The beat of a different drum - sound devices in Bronze Age Malta' in N. Vella et al (eds) *The Lure of the Antique* Leuven: Peeters: 205-218.
250 We were in Tunisia in 2010 not long before the Arab Spring began there and taxi drivers were keen to point out that it was local hip-hop on the radio, criticising the government and calling for freedom.
251 Porphyry (c. 300 CE) *Life of Pythagoras* canvases the possibility that the philosopher's father was Phoenician and that he learnt his maths and, one assumes, his music theory in the Phoenician homeland as well as at other points on his grand tour of the East.

# Conclusion

## The Phoenician Sonnets

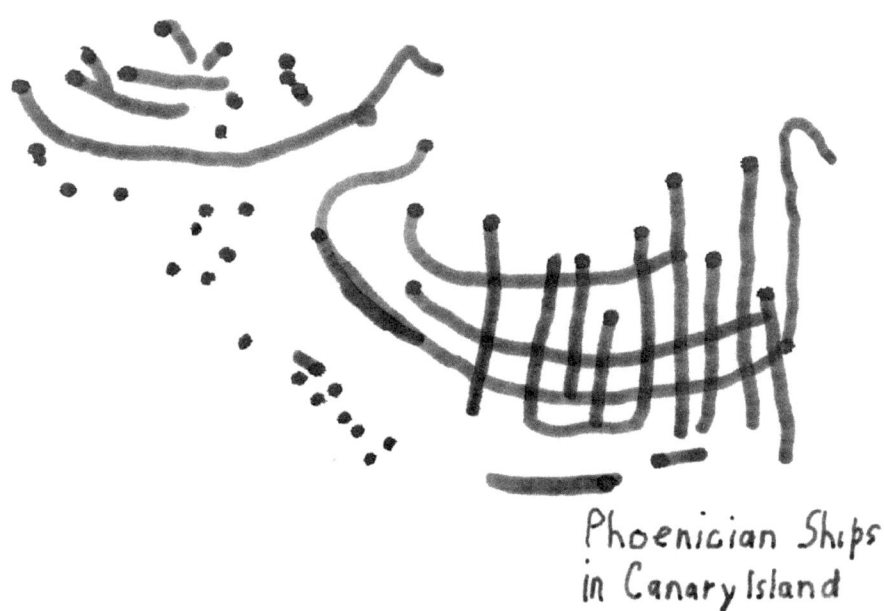

Phoenician Ships in Canary Island Rock Art

*Conclusion*

**Further Afield**

Rock art shows hippoi sailed to the Canary Isles[252]
But claims they made America are curious:
Some cults, designs and gods mimic Phoenician styles[253]
Yet detailed inscriptions proved to be spurious.[254]

North up Portugal's coast, past Sines and Lisbon
Where Eastern traces stay,[255] Himilco marked the way
To France, Cornwall and then the western isles beyond[256]
Where eastern roots to names like Sark and Scilly stay.[257]

And did the goddess give her name to Thanet Isle[258]
Which might explain the Punic coins found thereabouts?[259]
And did some go north with Carthaginian style
Into the Baltic Sea and sow their cultural sprouts
That may be seen in German language, gods and runes?[260]
How far did seas echo to the sound of Phoenician tunes?

---

252 A. Mederos & G. Escribano (1999) 'Pesquerías gaditanas' *Rivista di Studi Fenici* 27(1): 93-113.
253 Constance Irwin (1964) *Fair Gods and Stone Faces* London: W.H. Allen.
254 Maria Guzzo (1988) 'Did the Phoenicians Land in America?' in Moscati *The Phoenicians*: 570-572.
255 The Gaio Treasure in the Sines Municipal Museum (visited 2014) was found in the grave of an indigenous woman in 1966 and includes 'orientalising' artefacts, some from the East, some with local provenance (M.E. Aubet (2001) *The Phoenicians and the West* Cambridge: Cambridge University Press: 296; Culican 'Phoenicia and Phoenician Colonization': 534). Excavation of the cloisters behind Lisbon's Sé Cathedral has found Phoenician-influenced ceramics dating to the 8th century BCE.
256 Pliny *The Natural History:* XX.67; R.F. Avienus (c. 400 CE) *Ora Maritima:* 113-130, 380-389, 404-415.
257 SRQ=east, SL=rocks, for a summary of relevant evidence, see Caitlin Green's blog at https://www.caitlingreen.org/2015/04/thanet-tanit-and-the-phoenicians.html.
258 In eastern Kent, see Theo Vennemann (2006) 'The name of the Isle of Thanet' in A.J. Johnstone et al (eds), *Language and Text* Heidelberg: UWH: 345-348, 357-359.
259 D. Holman (2005) 'Iron Age Coinage and Settlement in East Kent' *Britannia* 36: 39-41. Caitlin Green shows the predominance of Punic coinage in Kent in her map at the blog post cited above.
260 Mailhammer & Vennemann *The Carthaginian North*.

*The Phoenician Sonnets*

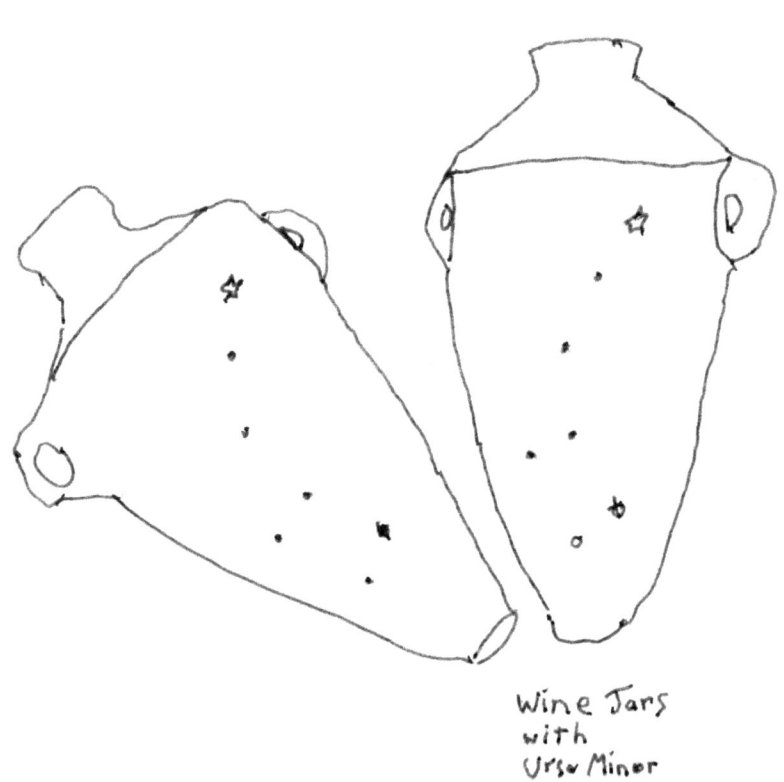

*Conclusion*

**Wine**

Wine's first made in Georgia, eight thousand years ago
But Phoenicians turned it into an industry:
They had a system to get the best grapes to grow,[261]
Made fine wine, branded it and sold it 'cross the sea.

They placed vineyards with care, avoiding too much sun
And tended vines with skill to maximise returns,
The precious juice was aged with timely precision
And made ready for trade in shapely airtight urns.

Those urns were mass-produced, distinctive amphorae,
And where Phoenicians went, markets were keen to buy,
From Byblos to Cadiz we come across these jars
And drink their descendants in restaurants and bars.
Let's toast fine wine and bless its ideology –
The Dionysus cult: from ritual to mythology.[262]

---

261 We know of their systematic approach to wine growing from Mago's treatise on agriculture which was saved from the sack of Carthage, translated by order of the Roman senate and quoted extensively by ancient authors. While Mago's book does not survive, his scientific approach to viniculture does, see J.A. Greene (1995) 'The Beginnings of Grape Cultivation and Wine Production in Phoenician/Punic North Africa', in P.E. McGovern et al *The Origins and Ancient History of Wine* Amsterdam: Gordon and Breach: 311-322.
262 A. Leonard (1995) 'Canaanite Jars and the Late Bronze Age Aegeo-Levantine Wine Trade' in McGovern et al *The Origins and Ancient History of Wine*: 233-254.

*Conclusion*

**Legacy**

We've seen how Phoenicians spread knowledge, gods and trade,
Culture glittered like phosphorescence in their wake,
From their earthly magic civilisation's made,
They taught the Greeks to think, the Romans to be great.

Their influence inspires our culture still today:
Turner painted Dido in Carthage resplendent[263]
And Flaubert's *Salammbo*[264] is back in e-game play[265]
While their political pull remains transcendent.[266]

For me, the Phoenicians, they gave my life a lift
When like *Waste Land's* Phlebas, poor health set me adrift,[267]
What started out as an academic pursuit
Then led to poetry and other literary loot.
The best things we found were the people of the route,
Their love of life and liberty, their spirit resolute.

---

263 J.M.W. Turner (1815) *Dido Building Carthage; or the Rise of the Carthaginian Empire* National Gallery, London; cf his (1817) *The Decline of the Carthaginian Empire*, Tate Britain.
264 Gustav Flaubert's 1862 novel tells of the revolt of Carthage's mercenary army after the city's defeat by Rome in the First Punic War.
265 *Salammbo: Battle for Carthage* was a 2003 Windows game by Dreamcatcher Interactive based on Flaubert's original novel and Philippe Druillet's sci-fi graphic novel trilogy (1980-6) reinterpreting Flaubert.
266 Quinn *In Search of the Phoenicians* outlines the mythological function of the Phoenicians in modern politics in Ireland, Britain and Lebanon.
267 'Phlebas the Phoenician, a fortnight dead' is the subject of the ten lines that survived Ezra Pound's editing of the original 92 lines to make up 'Death by Water', Part IV of T.S. Eliot *The Waste Land*, see particularly the 1971 facsimile edition from Faber and Faber, London: 54-69.

# The Phoenician Sonnets

*Conclusion*

**Phantasmagoria**

We've seen the Phoenicians most serious and straight,
Their brave adventuring is quite historical,
But there is something more to them, this is their fate,
They have a story more phantasmagorical.

It's strange out on the sea, especially at night,
Sailors easily drift away among the stars,
Carried aloft by bright gold-white celestial light,
The siren's song, the taste of salt, the wine in jars.

The hemp is always handy, its flowers delight,[268]
And next you're taking tea with Dido and the gods,
Then Hannibal and Heracles hove into sight,
Phoenicians here to help, exchanging knowing nods:
They've worked with elephants, used reason and sailed ships,
Have they something for us, to help steer from apocalypse?

---

268 Hemp was recovered with the boat now on display at the Baglio Anselmi Archaeological Museum in Marsala, Sicily (visited 2010).

## Essay
# The History of Phoenician-Greek Interaction

The amount, pathways and significance of cultural transmission from the Phoenicians to the ancient Greeks has been a vexed question for more than two centuries and will remain so well into the future. The possibility that a Semitic Middle Eastern, indeed Asian, culture like the Phoenicians informed, influenced and/or moulded the classical Graeco-Roman ideas that form the basis of Western civilization is an affront to many white people and most conservative politicians in Europe, America and Australia.

This is a flashpoint of the 'culture wars' and this essay seeks to lay out the evidence of Phoenician-Greek interaction in the Archaic Period preceding the Classical Age to establish that co-operation is the key to cultural development and whatever we thought Western civilisation was, it is just an aspect of a much larger and more complex Global civilisation. In particular I wish to clarify how the Phoenicians and Greeks worked together three thousand years ago to spread the literacy, expressive art, mindful spirituality, philosophy, science and democracy that mark out the best of humanity and, with appropriate criticism, development and adaptation, the best possibilities for our global future.[1]

A number of caveats need to be entered. The Phoenicians never considered themselves as such; it was a name that the Greeks gave them that only became a geographical descriptor in Roman times.[2]

---

1 For a comprehensive account of Phoenician contributions to western civilisation, see John C. Scott (2018) 'The Phoenicians and the Formation of the Western World' *Comparative Civilizations Review*. 78: 78/25-40.
2 Josephine Quinn (2017) *In Search of the Phoenicians* Princeton: Princeton University Press.

## The History of Phoenician-Greek Interaction

Both Phoenicians and Greeks traded slaves, oppressed women and sacrificed children.³ The Phoenicians had colonialist tendencies and while they started out as relatively peaceful traders, they ended with a feared naval fleet and their descendants in Carthage ran a most efficient military machine. By contrast the Greeks were out-right war mongers with imperialist aspirations.⁴

With these foundations one can appreciate why many on the planet are concerned about the wisdom, or possibility, of Western civilisation. Let us, for the moment, put these negative issues aside while we consider the role of the Phoenicians in introducing some key positive concepts to the Greeks. A final caveat here, I make no claim that the Phoenicians generated all the ideas we are about to discuss, rather they listened carefully to the notions they came across in their trade and travel to Egypt, Mesopotamia, Israel and Syria and transmitted them further afield and certainly across the Mediterranean.

### The Issue

Until the 1820s ancient writers such as Herodotus and Thucydides were generally taken at their word on the significant contribution of Phoenician culture to the development of ancient Greece. Bernal sketches how this Ancient model persisted, with some critique by Plutarch among others, from antiquity to early modern times.⁵ Then, first in Germany and later in English-speaking academies, the contribution of Semitic Phoenicians was sidelined by the overpowering influence of the Aryan model. This model argued that the flourishing

---

3 Greeks sacrificed children? At least it happens without comment in its foundational mythology: Agamemnon sacrifice his daughter for good winds on his way to Troy in Euripides (c. 407 BCE) *Iphigenia in Aulis;* Erechtheus, the mythical king of Athens must sacrifice his daughter to save the city, see Joan Breton Connelly (2014) *The Parthenon Enigma* New York: Knopf.
4 David Pritchard (ed) (2010), *War, Democracy and Culture in Classical Athens,* Cambridge: Cambridge University Press.
5 Martin Bernal (1991) *Black Athena: The Afroasiatic Roots of Classical Civilisation, Volume I: The Fabrication of Ancient Greece 1785-1985* London: Vintage.

of Greece in classical times was entirely the result of the arrival of Dorians, a branch of the Indo-European people who spread their 'purposeful' ways from India to Germany and England, and Greece.

The rise of political anti-Semitism contributed to the growth of the Aryan model during the 19$^{th}$ century and up to the World War Two.[6] By the 1930s, Phoenician art was derided in Western academies as derivative and the discovery that there had been a Greek enclave in Al Mina near the mouth of the Orontes from 800 BCE allowed the implication that all Eastern influence on Greece (alphabet, art, myths and techniques to produce orientalising luxuries) could be 'attributed almost entirely to the initiative of the Greeks in the Levantine'.[7] Even after the War, classicists dismissed not only the influence, but even the presence, of Phoenicians in the Greek sphere in the archaic period.[8]

Against this attempt to dismiss the Phoenicians from history, Coldstream argued, at first tentatively in the 60s and then more authoritatively in the 80s, that the Phoenicians are most unlikely to have avoided the Aegean, the most direct route on their way to their increasingly well-attested presence in the Western Mediterranean. Further he points to the archaeological finds in Athens, Euboea, Crete and Kos that pre-date the settlement at Al Mina and suggest the presence of enclaves of Phoenician craftsmen working and training locals in these areas before 800 BCE and Rhodes not long after.[9] Then followed a range of archaeological and epigraphic work that clearly established the presence of Phoenicians across the Mediterranean preceding the Greek classic period. Let us now consider the inter-

---

6 ibid: 393-399.
7 J.N. Coldstream (1982) 'Greeks and Phoenicians in the Aegean' in H.G. Niemeyer (ed) *Phonizier in Westen* Mainz: Zaben: 262.
8 See, for example R. Carpenter (1958) 'Phoenicians in the West' *American Journal of Archaeology* 62: 35-53.
9 Coldstream 'Greeks and Phoenicians in the Agean': 268. A contention supported by R. Drews (1979) 'Phoenicians, Carthage and the Spartan Eunomia', *American Journal of Philology*, 100(1): 46 and J. Goody (1996) *The East in the West*. Cambridge: Cambridge University Press: 250. For contact dates, see E. Lipinski (2004) *Itineraria Phoenicia* Leuven: Peeters: 155.

cultural work that occurred between Greeks and Phoenicians in that time and, particularly, in these enclaves.

**Alphabet and Literacy**
It is generally conceded that the Phoenician alphabet informed the creation of the Greek alphabet. While at the height of the Aryan model some sought to challenge this now uncontentious point, the order of the Greek letters and their shape clearly point to their Phoenician origins as claimed by Herodotus in the classical period.[10] All the Greek variant alphabets have the same vowels and a core group of consonants which suggests a single moment of invention before the prototype alphabet is dispersed around Greece and various consonants are introduced or adapted regionally.[11]

We are not sure whether that moment of invention occurred in the east (Al Mina, for example), Crete or the eastern Aegean but we can easily imagine the off-spring of a mixed marriage in an enclave in one of those areas applying the Phoenician parent's literacy to their Greek parent's language, using some redundant letters to distinguish between similar words (bat, bet, bit, bot, but) and then teaching the skill to traders or their children who spread it across the Mediterranean. The earliest Greek inscriptions are dated around 750 BCE and the alphabet appears to have spread quickly because there are examples of probable eighth-century origin that appear in Attica, Euboea, Aegina, Ithaka, Thera, Smyrna, Rhodes and Pithecusae.[12]

Many have argued that the Greek alphabet must have developed shortly before the inscriptions appeared but regional letter variations, the different direction of Phoenician and Greek

---

10 Herodotus (430 BCE) *The Histories:* V.58-61.
11 W. Waal (2018) 'On the "Phoenician Letters": The case for an early transmission of the Greek alphabet from an archaeological, epigraphic and linguistic perspective' *Aegean Studies:* 1: 83-125.
12 A. Snodgrass (1971) *The Dark Age of Greece: An Archaeological Survey of the Eleventh to Eighth Centuries B.C.* Edinburgh: Edinburgh University Press: 421.

writing (the former right to left, the latter left to right) and the predominantly private uses of writing that are apparent when inscriptions first appear in the 8$^{th}$ century lead Waal and others to suggest earlier origins of the Greek alphabet that spread and developed on fragile media that does not survive.[13] While Bernal argues for transmission as early as the 14$^{th}$ century BCE, Waal cites recent linguistic and archaeological evidence to date it to around 1000 BCE which points to extended contact between Phoenicians and Greeks during what is described as 'the dark ages'.

The utility of the alphabet developed with practice in both the Phoenician and Greek spheres and points to the continuing significance of literacy on social development today. Writing began as an aid to recording and managing trade among the commercial class but as more people learnt literacy, the alphabet could be put to other purposes. Early Phoenician uses include the identification of personal property (cups, arrows etc) and the commemoration of leaders and war. Additional early Greek uses include the promulgation of laws (in Chios and Dreros, Crete for example) and setting down oral traditions that bear the imprint of eastern origins (*The Epic of Gilgamesh*) in texts that continue to form the basis of our literature: the work of Homer and Hesiod.

Thus, we see the function of literacy as a civilising force: allowing individuals to define their own domain, learn the social fabric, participate in their political communities and open their imaginations. Further the alphabet provides opportunities for analytic and abstract thought that goes from matching elements in the production process (eg the pre-fab boat, the furniture kit), through the ordering of data (by alphabetisation) to the manufacture of new ideas (via neologism and portmanteau words).[14] In our digital age where audio-visual communication competes

---

13 Waal op cit.
14 The McLuhanite argument for the contribution of the alphabet to abstract and analytic thought and thus western civilisation is summarised in R.K. Logan (2004) *The Alphabet Effect* Cresskill: Hampton Press. Its ethno-centric bias has been criticised though the alphabet's systematising effects are apparent.

with reading and writing for peoples' attention, literacy remains significant not only in alphabetical contexts where its critical uses are important but also in computer/visual contexts where digital literacy allows high levels of participation in social communication.

**Expressive Art**
While questions have been raised about the originality and origins of Phoenician art, the Orientalising period saw them introduce their workmanship, skills and techniques into Greece and across the Mediterranean.[15] Many key motifs used by the Phoenicians come from high culture of Egypt and the Semitic East (particularly Assyria) and their eclecticism was a useful contribution to the development of art then and now. The Orientalising period is generally given as 750-650 BCE and the Phoenicians played a significant role in transporting figurative and expressive art to the Greeks during this period and earlier. The Minoans and Myceneans had figurative styles that had been lost in the Dark Ages after the fall of palace societies. Geometric decoration was predominant for many hundreds of years. Phoenicians provided the prompt to assist Greek artists find a dynamic realism again. Excavations have found Phoenician prototypes alongside local copies in a range of locales including Cyprus, Euboea, Crete, Rhodes, Kos and Athens in a fashion that suggests migrant craftsmen coming from the East, settling in Greece, creating workshops and passing skills and insights to locals.[16]

Clear connections between Phoenician influence and Greek mastery can be made: on Crete where a hemispherical bronze bowl with a Phoenician inscription found in the cemetery near Knossos[17]

---

15 Walter Burkert (1992) *The Orientalizing Revolution: Near Eastern influence on Greek culture in the early archaic age* Cambridge, Mass: Harvard University Press.
16 For a recent systematic account of the earliest Phoenician finds in Greece, see Giorgos Bourogiannis (2018) 'The Phoenician presence in the Aegean during the Early Iron Age: trade, settlement and cultural interaction' *Rivista di Studi Fenici* 46: 43–88.
17 R. Osborne (2009) *Greece in the Making, 1200-479BC* London: Routledge: 63.

presages the fine metalwork in the stunning shields found in the cave shrine on Mt Ida[18]; on the Ionian coast where eastern ivories of the tree of life and attendant animals, often goats, prompt the creation of pots in the 'Wild Goat' style with exquisite detail and naturalistic style;[19] and in Athens where a Phoenician bronze bowl and other objects found in the Kerameikos cemetery[20] and 'a false scarab' seal with bearded face and hawks of 'great beauty and delicately rendered' from a tomb southeast of the city,[21] all dated as early as the 9$^{th}$ century BCE, are clear precursors to Athenian mastery of the human figure, first on vases and then in the monumental sculpture of the classical period including the Elgin Marbles of the Parthenon frieze.

So, while Phoenician art is derivative in borrowing Egyptian and Assyrian motifs, the skill in representing those figurative images, the concentration on technique to draw the viewer into the experience of the art and the representation of the dynamic moment of action, all underpin the artistic expressiveness of the most excellent classical Greek art that continues to inspire us today. Further the freedom of thought inherent in the eclectic style that drew disparate motifs and techniques together to make an original statement, remind us of not only 20$^{th}$ century collage, surrealism and postmodernism but also contemporary digital exploration drawing together disparate images into a comprehensive, dynamic flow.

**Mindful Spirituality**

Phoenicians also assisted in the transmission of spirituality from East to West, most obviously in the personalities and proclivities of gods but also in the life of the soul or, in non-religious terms, the well-being of the mind. Since Neolithic times Greece had been open to western

---

18 J.N. Coldstream (1982) 'Greeks and Phoenicians in the Aegean' in H.G. Niemeyer (ed) *Phonizier in Westen* Mainz: Zaben: 268.
19 As is apparent in the Rhodes Archaeological Museum.
20 Osborne 2009: 62; 158.
21 David Robinson (1949) 'The Robinson Collection of Greek Gems, Seals, Rings, and Earrings' *Hesperia* Supplement 8: 311.

Asian culture: not only agriculture, metal-working and artistic fashions but also religious institutions and mythology. Over the last sixty years scholars have increasingly become aware of links between the mythological literatures of Mesopotamia, Anatolia, Canaan and Israel and the Greek mythology as recorded and developed by Hesiod, the Homeric epics, the lyric poets and Aeschylus.[22]

For example, the Mesopotamian gods Ishtar and Tammuz inspired their Phoenician counterparts, Astarte and Baal, who in turn inspired Greek Mythology. While Astarte as goddess of love and war has a direct connection to the Greek goddess Aphrodite and their devotees have shared temples in Crete and Kythera, Baal has a more convoluted relationship with the Greek gods. As a weather god Baal was often connected to thunder like the Greek god Zeus, but his power over the weather grew to encompass the cyclical processes of nature and he became an archetypal dying and resurrecting god, returning from the underworld to bring Earth back to life each spring. Jessie Weston traces this aspect of Baal back to Tammuz and then further back to the Indian Rig Veda and forward to Christianity and the story of Perceval and the Fisher King in the legend of the Holy Grail.[23] Each Phoenician city's Baal had a local rebirth cult that contributed different aspects to the Greek pantheon: Byblos's Baal, known as Adonis, carried spring rebirth into the Greek pantheon, the Baal of Sidon was the healing god, Eshmun with symbolic connections to the Greek Asclepius (both represented by a staff entwined by two snakes) and Melqart, the Baal and protector of Tyre finds a new life in the Greek sphere as the semi-divine but very influential Heracles whose twelve labours represent the superiority of reason and determination over tradition, superstition and the chthonic.[24]

---

22 M.L. West (1997) *The East Face of Helicon: West Asiatic Elements in Greek Poetry and Myth* Oxford: Clarendon Press.
23 J.L. Weston (1920) *From Ritual to Romance* Cambridge: Cambridge University Press.
24 Glenn Markoe (2000) *Phoenicians* London: The British Museum Press: 116-9.

But beyond the social connections with the gods played out in spring rebirth festivals and temple observances, Phoenicians had a personal relationship with often specialised gods which is evident in Jonah's observation that 'each cried out to his own god'.[25] These specialised religions indicate how individual connection with the divine could develop, in the context of the personal freedom required for distributed, remote commercial activity, into an appreciation of the self as the location of judgement not just for business purposes but for spiritual and ethical decisions as well.

Self-awareness was not just a goal in itself, but rather something sought after in the psycho-moral work required to care for oneself. Transmuting divine connections in the materialist world, this work was philosophically systematised as stoicism by Zeno of Citium (Kition), himself a trader and the product of the Phoenician community on Cyprus. The techniques of the Stoics include participation in deep reflection to place past and future actions in the context of one's values and goals and the contemplation of nature to place one's minor existence in the greater cosmos. Mindful stoicism continues to be a useful tool for realising one's spirituality in the modern world.[26]

**Science and Philosophy**

Along with trade, alphabet, art and religion, there is even evidence that, informed by the work of the Mesopotamians and Egyptians and their own pragmatic approach, the Phoenicians carried embryonic scientific and philosophical ideas into the Greek sphere of influence and contributed to the systematic thinking that precedes the rise of science and philosophy.

In antiquity Phoenicians were famed for their practical approach to problem-solving: Herodotus points to their pragmatic methods

---

25 Jonah 1:5; see also A.J. Brody (1999) *Each Man Cried Out to his God: The Specialized Religion of Canaanite and Phoenician Seafarers* Atlanta: Scholars Press.
26 Brigid Delaney (2022) *Reasons Not to Worry: How to be Stoic in Chaotic Times* Sydney: Allen & Unwin.

## The History of Phoenician-Greek Interaction

in besting the Persians as they dug their section of the Mt Athos canal more efficiently and built a sturdier bridge across the Hellespont; Xenophon extols their systematic approach to laying out sails, tools and other necessities on their ships.[27] Phoenicians are also credited with introducing nocturnal navigation by steering by the north star, Polaris from the constellation Ursa Minor and they had a series of technical and scientific achievements in metallurgy, ceramic production, glassmaking, dyeing, food production, textile production and carpentry.[28]

Where did this practical philosophy come from? Philo of Byblos tells of Sanchuniathon of Beirut, who wrote as early as the Trojan War in the 12th century BCE, that life came from an egg generated in moist slime and suggests that we have material rather than purely divine origins.[29] Others argue that the texts attributed to Sanchuniathon come from the Hellenistic period (starting 332 BCE) because its 'structure, themes and rationalising euhemerism' (that is: interpretation of myths as based on real events) are too advanced to be dated any earlier.[30] But perhaps that original text was older, indeed contemporaneous with similar ideas found in Ugarit from around the time of the Trojan War, and the Phoenicians had a realistic approach all along that they transmitted into the Greek sphere before Hesiod's time (700 BCE) when he wrote a materialistic account of the gods in his *Theogyny*. Pherecydes, the first Greek prose writer, described a complex reality of earth, time, watery chaos and unity, admittedly with divine influence and so also bridged the mythic and the material as Hesiod

---

27 Herodotus *The Histories:* VII.23; VII.33-5; Xenophon (c. 360 BCE) *Oeconomicus:* VIII.
28 P. Bartoloni (1988) 'Ships and Navigation' in Sabatino Moscati (ed) (1988) *The Phoenicians* Milan: Bompiani: 72; P. Bartoloni (1995) 'Techniques and Sciences' in V. Kring (ed) *La civilisation phenicienne et punique: Manuel de recherche* Leiden: Brill: 354-61.
29 Albert I. Baumgarten (1981) *The Phoenician History of Philo of Byblos: A Commentary* Leiden: Brill: 6-7.
30 Baumgarten *The Phoenician History of Philo of Byblos:* 96. Quinn *In Search of the Phoenicians*: 146.

## The Phoenician Sonnets

did. He 'is said to have had no teacher, but to have used... the "secret books of the Phoenicians"'.[31]

The Phoenicians were in the right place at the right time to learn a proto-scientific approach to medicine from Egypt where the 'famous Edwin Smith papyrus' (dated to around 1600 BCE) analyses forty-eight cases of clinical surgery in a systematic fashion 'divided into the title, the examination, the diagnosis, the treatment and explanations of difficult medical terms' and indicates the use of simple, physical treatments, generally avoiding magic and pointing to something more than folk medicine and closer to the empirical methods employed by Hippocrates and his acolytes.[32]

They also learnt maths and astronomy from the Assyrians and Babylonians who were adept at arithmetical calculations, algebra and quadratic equations. These mathematical skills were most useful in managing the astronomical data produced, for example: by observations of Venus recorded on the Ammisaduqa tablet from 1581 BCE; and by eclipses recorded from 747 BCE.[33] The mix of maths and astronomy allowed the Babylonians to make accurate predictions of lunar eclipses and reasonable predictions of solar eclipses in techniques used by the Greek Thales in Miletus to establish the power of scientific prediction.

Thales, the first of antiquity's Seven Sages played a key role in the transition of scientific and philosophical ideas. Of Phoenician heritage, Thales travelled to the Egypt and the east and returned with a practical approach that saw him make significant achievements in political, military and business spheres as well as arguing for a material metaphysics based, like Phoenicians before him, on water.[34] Thales moulded Phoenician

---

31 West *Early Greek Philosophy and the Orient*: 1-3.
32 G.E.R. Lloyd (1970) *Early Greek Science: Thales to Aristotle* London: Chatto & Windus: 4;7.
33 Jöran Friberg (2007) *Amazing Traces of a Babylonian Origin in Greek Mathematics* River Edge: World Scientific.
34 J. Barnes (2001) *Early Greek Philosophy.* (2nd rev. ed.) London: Penguin: 9-17. B. L. Van der Waerden (1961) *Science Awakening* (trans A. Dresden) New York: Oxford University Press: 5.

insights and established the Greek discourse on materialistic nature that was pursued by his student Anaximander who discerned the importance of the infinite in understanding the size and complexity of the material cosmos.[35]

Pythagoras from Samos near Miletus, whose father was reputedly Phoenician, also travelled to Egypt and the east and returned with a doctrine of reincarnation and a theoretical appreciation of mathematics that saw him, or his school, derive not only the famous theorem but also the theory of proportionality, that earth was a sphere and the mathematical nature of music.[36] Heraclitus from Ephesus, also near Miletus, argued for the unity of the cosmos while embracing the dynamic realities of material change.[37] This materialist tradition was refined into the rational atomism of Leucippus, who may have been born in Miletus,[38] and his pupil Democritus that remained influential until the relatively recent discovery of sub-atomic particles (by J.J. Thomson, 1897).

In the Socratic dialogues *Meno* and *Phaedo,* Plato promotes a shift away from materialism to idealism that comes to fruition in *The Republic's* Theory of Forms, outlined in the Allegory of the Cave, which argues that immutable ideas, and not the material world apprehended by the senses, are the best path to reality. It was Plato's student, Aristotle, who clarified the distinctive contributions of idealism and materialism in understanding reality and, by returning to Thales and other crucial pre-Socratics, made a major contribution with his own empirical research to the development of a materialist scientific method and natural philosophy.[39]

---

35 Barnes *Early Greek Philosophy:* 18-23.
36 ibid: 28-35; on father see Porphyry (c. 300 CE) *Life of Pythagoras*
37 Barnes *Early Greek Philosophy:* 48-73.
38 ibid: 201.
39 Anna Makolkin (2016) 'Phoenician Cosmology as a Proto-base for Greek Materialism, Naturalist Philosophy and Aristotelianism' *Biocosmology* 6:3&4; A.M. Leroi (2014) *The Lagoon: How Aristotle Invented Science* London: Bloomsbury.

The question of the Phoenician contribution to the development of philosophy and science is set against the contemporary debate between histories of the sciences and models of global history that problematize the traditional western claim to its scientific dominance as the natural order of things and suggests an approach that sees a multiplicity of sciences – world science - taking form in the context of global conflicts, interactions and political agendas, appreciating the vital role of cross-cultural interaction and the trading of ideas.[40] The challenge is not to homogenise science but to encourage communication between different scientific cultures to produce mutually beneficial new possibilities, the very role the Phoenicians played. The Phoenicians' practical approach to theory, their ability to take eclectic ideas and meld them into new formations and their cross-cultural approach all suggest useful future directions for philosophy and science.

**Democracy**

Previous work has explored the Phoenician contribution to development of democratic ideas and their role in transmitting them to the Greeks.[41] That work is summarised here and the opportunity is taken to also consider an old source afresh to see how Phoenicians played a crucial role at a key moment in Athens' transition from tyranny to mature democracy.

The 'egalitarian mutuality' that is evident in tribal decision-making suggest the roots of democracy lie deep in human history.[42] 'Primitive democracy' moderated the power of kings in the earliest cities in Mesopotamia,[43] India, Hittite Anatolia and the Syro-

---

40 S. Sivasundaram and M. Elshakry (eds) (2012) *Science, Race and Imperialism* London: Chatto and Pickering.
41 Stephen Stockwell (2011), 'Before Athens: Early Popular Government in Phoenicia and Greek City States' in B. Isakhan & S. Stockwell *The Secret History of Democracy* London: Palgrave MacMillan: 35-48 ; Stephen Stockwell (2012) 'Israel and Phoenicia' in B. Isakhan & S. Stockwell *Edinburgh Companion to the History of Democracy* Edinburgh: Edinburgh University Press: 71-81.
42 Kenneth Maddock (1974) *The Australian Aborigines* Ringwood: Penguin: 166.
43 Thorkild Jacobsen (1970 [1943]) 'Primitive Democracy in Ancient Mesopotamia' in W. L. Moran (ed), *Toward the Image of Tammuz* Massachusetts: Harvard University Press: 157-70.

Palestinian region.⁴⁴ Phoenician trade to these areas would have exposed them to this concept. Their links to Israel introduced them to the law of Moses and its principle that as a covenant between God and the people, the rule of that law extended to leaders like Moses himself, requiring his deference to the assembly of the people and care that the letter of the law is obeyed – there is no royal prerogative.⁴⁵ In the 14th century BCE *Amarna Letters* there are examples of the people of Phoenician cities exercising their sovereignty; in the 10th century BCE *Report of Wenamun* the king of Byblos defers to the city's assembly; in the late 9th century a people's uprising splits the ruling dynasty in Tyre and forces Dido to flee and found Carthage;⁴⁶ after that the authority of Phoenician kings wanes even further so by the 7th century BCE Tyre's treaty with Assyria is specifically in conjunction with both the city's king and council of elders as equal partners; and by 572 BCE, after the siege of Babylonian Nebuchadnezzar II, Tyre is, for a period, ruled by suffetes or judges, who were perhaps elected.

Phoenicians were clearly experimenting with their own forms of proto-democracy by the time they were having an orientalising effect on the Greeks and my analysis of Eric Robinson's *The First Democracies* reveals that of the twenty Greek city-states with various experience of popular free rule before 508 BCE when Kleisthenes' reforms introduced mature democracy to Athens, four-fifths of those were on or adjacent to the Phoenician trading route.⁴⁷ Then there is the case of Sparta which had trade and cultural connections with the Phoenicians and, as Aristotle and some modern commentators point out, a system of quasi-democratic government similar to Tyre's colony, Carthage.⁴⁸

---

44  E.W. Robinson (1997) *The First Democracies* Stuttgart: Franz Steiner Verlag: 21-22.
45  C.U. Wolf (1947) 'Traces of Primitive Democracy in Ancient Israel' *Journal of Near Eastern Studies* 6(2): 98-108
46  G. Rawlinson (1889) *History of Phoenicia* London: Longmans, Green and Co: 205.
47  Stockwell 'Before Athens': 43-6.
48  ibid: 46-7.

Taken together these historical moments provide a suggestive case for Phoenician-Greek interaction contributing to the development of democracy. Kurt Raaflaub has laid down the challenge to explain exactly how the Phoenician roots were 'transplanted' into the Greek polis.[49] Any response will have to address the Phoenician contribution to the emergence of democracy in the most important case of all, Athens. As discussed above, there is evidence of Phoenician contact with Athens from the 9th century BCE but the question remains about the exact nature of the Phoenician contribution to the development of democracy there.

Solon's proto-democratic reforms of the Athenian constitution around 595 BCE not only forgave debts and ended debt slavery but also opened the assembly to the lower classes, even if they were not able to run for office – so the aristocrats continued to dominate the polis.[50] Solon was not only an aristocratic poet but also a trader and so had the opportunity to travel east and meet Phoenicians at ports and in their homeland. At this point Athens was surrounded by a number of city-states, influenced by the Phoenicians, that were already experimenting with new forms of increasingly democratic government. The Athenians cannot have avoided the indirect contribution by the Phoenicians in their decision to devise a more egalitarian system of governance.

Unfortunately, the reforms of Solon did not have a permanent impact and Athens degenerated back into dynastic tyranny. Strikingly, the existing historical record shows Phoenician leadership in a passionate attempt to overthrow that tyranny which signalled its brittle fragility, its eventual demise and the emergence of mature Athenian democracy. The response to Raaflaub's challenge has been hiding in plain sight in Herodotus's *The Histories*.

---

49 K.A. Raaflaub (2005) 'Poets, lawgivers, and the beginnings of political reflection in archaic Greece' in C. Rowe & M. Schofield *The Cambridge History of Greek and Roman Political Thought* Cambridge: Cambridge University Press: 52.
50 ibid: 39-42.

Peisistratos was a relatively benign dictator who ruled Athens intermittently between 561 and 527 BCE and did much to unify the city and draw the people together, particularly through the introduction of the Panathenaic festival.[51] At Peisistratos's death his sons, Hippias and Hipparchus took power, Hippias as leader and Hipparchus as his cultural enforcer, for example as marshal of the Panathenaic festival. The younger Peisistratids did not have their father's softer touch and opposition to their tyranny intensified. It was on the day of the Panathenaic festival that Harmodius and Aristogiton set out to assassinate Hippias but seeing him chatting in a friendly fashion with a fellow conspirator they assumed that they had been betrayed and coming across Hipparchus marshalling the parade, they killed him instead.[52] While Thucydides suggests the attack was motivated by an unrequited love affair between Hipparchus and Harmodius and subsequent subtle family insults, he nevertheless confirms that the leader, Hippias was the original target and that the assassins hoped other citizens would come to their aid in an impromptu uprising to bring about freedom and the rule of the people.

It is Herodotus who points out that the assassins came from the Gephyraei clan, 'descendants of those who came with Cadmus to what is now Boeotia (and who) took refuge in Athens where they were received into the community... I myself have looked into the matter and find that they were really Phoenicians'.[53] Herodotus leaves the assassination narrative at that point to extol the Phoenicians contribution to the development of writing and trace the Gephyraei's travels to Athens 'where they have certain temples set apart for their own special use... one of them is the temple of Demeter Achaeia, in which secret rites are performed.'[54] Demeter

---

51 G.R. Stanton (1990) *Athenian Politics C. 800-500 B.C.: A Sourcebook*. London: Routledge: 65-86.
52 Thucydides (c. 410 BCE) *History of the Peloponnesian War*. VI.53-60.
53 Herodotus *The Histories*: V.57-58.
54 Herodotus *The Histories*: V.61.

was the goddess of the Harvest and the Earth itself, though in ways that complemented rather than competed with Gaia. She gave humanity the knowledge of agricultural husbandry and the laws that encouraged people to live in harmony with each other and with nature. Demeter was central to the highly secret rituals of the Eleusinian Mysteries which, in a rare moment of egalitarianism for aristocratic Athens of that period, welcomed men, women and slaves to join together in devotions that ensured the rebirth of the Earth and its fecundity.[55] As we saw above these practices had Phoenician precursors in the ceremonies around the annual rebirth of Baal. The Gephyraei, as Phoenician outsiders, were proponents of equality for Athens taking all means available in its pursuit. The actions of Harmodius and Aristogiton are clearly foundational to the democracy that subsequently emerged as the drinking song recorded by Athenaeus of Naucratis seven centuries later indicate:

> I'll wreathe my sword in myrtle bough,
> Like the sword that laid the tyrant low,
> When patriots, burning to be free,
> To Athens gave equality.
> Harmodius, hail! Though reft of breath,
> Thou ne'er shalt feel the stroke of death...
> I'll wreathe the sword in myrtle bough,
> The sword that laid Hipparchus low...
> You dared to set your country free,
> And gave her laws equality.[56]

The assassination did not immediately lead to democracy but as Hippias became more paranoid, the tyranny was exacerbated making

---

[55] K. Servi (2000) *Greek Mythology* Athens: Ekdotike Athenon: 36-37.
[56] Athenaeus of Naucratis (c. 200 CE) *The Deipnosophists or Banquet of the Learned*: 15.50.x-xiii.

Kleisthenes' c. 508 BCE democratic reforms very easy to introduce. There is something important in the Phoenician contribution to democracy that speaks across the millennia to us today particularly as we face rising authoritarianism and despotism around the world. There was no overriding Phoenician ideology that insisted on one perfect formula for democracy that was guaranteed to work every time. Instead there was commitment to the possibility that people knew their own minds and could rule themselves more fairly, justly and effectively than self-appointed kings, aristocrats and oligarchs. As people today become jaded with the failures of democracy, with politicians elected by the people selling out to monied and vested interests at a derisively cheap price, with manufactured rhetoric in sound bites and on social media devoid of conviction, with systems and ideas caught in the past, there is an opportunity for people to seize the day and remake democracy on their own terms with the passion that the Phoenicians brought to Athens.

## Conclusion

The preceding discussion casts doubt on the Aryan model of Greek history that sought to minimise Semitic Phoenician contributions to the literacy, expressive art, spiritual mindfulness, science, philosophy and democracy that were at the core of classical Greek achievement. The case has been put for a revised Ancient model of Greek civilisation that recognises the complexity of cultural influences (not just Phoenician but Dorian, Egyptian, Mesopotamian, Minoan, Mycenean and indigenous too) which contributed to the formation of classical Greece. The escape from the ethno-centrism of the Aryan model allows us to accept the positive aspects of Greece's significant contribution to world civilisation, critique the sexism, racism, slavery and other negative issues that were part of classical societies and develop new (and old) ideas and strategies to respond to the on-going challenge of global enlightenment. In brief, western civilisation must not be ceded to conservative ideology because, while many mistakes have been made, it contains a core of progressive ideas that helps us imagine the global civilisation that we need to counter over-population, unfair wealth distribution and climate change.

Educators in the west are often encouraged by politicians and pundits to celebrate western civilization as a means to instil pride, enthusiasm and determination into their students but the Phoenicians left traces that speak across time to warn us that things are not so simple. Coming from the Middle East more than three thousand years ago, working across geographical, linguistic and cultural boundaries, embracing difference and responding to it productively, the experience of the Phoenicians suggests civilization as a global enterprise based on purposeful contact, mutual respect and a joy at learning new things from others.

Of course Phoenician-Greek interactions were not universally positive. There were mutual suspicions from the outset that are clear in Homer and other surviving Greek texts. Eventually there were alliances with other parties that led to military conflict between former friends such as the battles of Alalia (535 BCE) and Salamis (480 BCE). Finally the Greeks under Alexander conquered the Phoenician homeland and ushered in a period of Hellenization that saw Phoenician culture, as such, disappear.

Yet in a world history often told in terms of emperors and their armies, great men and decisive moments, the Phoenicians are different. They were better known for their emporiums than as progenitors of empire, much more successful as salesmen than as soldiers, prospering more in their commercial endeavours from corporate effort and seasonal return than imperial prescription and continuing colonisation. While the Phoenicians were far from perfect, there is much to be learnt from them about building a global economy of goods and ideas that fosters humanity, nurtures the planet and finds alternatives to conflict and war.

# Museums and Selected Sites Visited

**2002**
Agora Museum, Athens
Acropolis and Pnyx, Athens
Heraklion Archaeological Museum
Knossos Archaeological Site
Chios Archaeological Museum
Erythrae Archaeological Site
Metropolitan Museum, New York

**2008**
Istanbul Archaeology Museums
Topkapi Palace Museum
National Museum of Damascus
Palmyra Archaeological Museum

**2010**
Carthage Museum and Byrsa Hill
Carthage Tophet and Punic Ports
Bardo Museum, Tunis
Kerkouane Archaeological
 Museum and Site
Whitaker Museum, Motya
Baglio Anselmi Archaeological
 Museum, Marsala

Paolo Orsi Archaeological
 Museum, Syracuse
National Archaeological Museum
 of Sibaritide and Park
National Archaeological
 Museum of Metaponto
Olympia Archaeological Museum
Sparta Archaeological Museum
National Archaeological
 Museum, Athens
Naxos Archaeological Museum
Kos Archaeological Museum
Rhodes Archaeological Museum
Larnaka District Archaeological Museum
Pierides Museum, Larnaka
Kition Archaeological Site
National Museum of Beirut
American University of Beirut Museum
Tyre Archaeological Sites
Eshmun Temple Archaeological
 Site, Sidon
Byblos Crusader Castle and
 Archaeological Site
Ugarit Archaeological Site
National Museum of Aleppo

## The Phoenician Sonnets

2014
National Etruscan Museum,
  Villa Giulia, Rome
Giovanni Barracco Museum of
  Ancient Sculpture, Rome
National Archaeological
  Museum, Caligari
Tuvixeddu Archaeological
  Park, Caligari
Nora and Tharros Archaeological Sites
Archaeological Museum Ferruccio
  Barreca, Sant'Antioco
National Museum Giovanni
  Antonio Sanna, Sassari
National Archaeological
  Museum, Madrid
Lisbon Sé Cathedral
  Archaeological Site
National Museum of
  Archaeology, Lisbon
Navy Museum, Lisbon
Sines Municipal Museum
Cadiz Museum
Puppet Theatre Archaeological
  Site, Cadiz
Huelva Museum
Archaeological Museum of Seville
Archaeological Museum of Cordoba
Basement, Picasso Museum, Malaga
Cave of the Seven Palaces, Alumenacar

Kasbah Museum, Tangiers
Lixus Archaeology Site
Volubilis Archaeology Site
Archaeology Museum, Rabat
Sidi Mohammed ben Abdallah
  Museum, Essaouira

2015
R.D. Milns Antiquities Museum,
  University of Queensland
Abbey Museum of Art and
  Archaeology, Caboolture

2016
Neues Museum, Berlin
Louvre, Paris
Petit Palace, Paris
British Museum
Champollion Museum, Figeac

2019
National Museum of Ireland -
  Archaeology
World Museum, Liverpool
Museum of the Arab World, Paris
National Archaeological
  Museum of Florence
National Archaeological
  Museum of Naples

## Museums and Selected Sites Visited

Archaeological Museum of
  Pithecusae, Villa Arbusto, Ischia
Herculaneum Archaeological Site
Archaeology Museum of
  Catalonia, Barcelona

2021
Nicholson Collection, Chau
  Chak Wing Museum,
  University of Sydney

2022
Ashmolean Museum of Art and
  Archaeology, Oxford
Israel Museum
HaMizgaga Museum of
  Archaeology and Glass, Dor
Hecht Museum, University of Haifa
National Maritime Museum, Haifa

# Top Ten Phoenician Books

George Rawlinson (1889) *History of Phoenicia* London: Longmans, Green and Co.
Constance Irwin (1964) *Fair Gods and Stone Faces* London: W.H. Allen.
Glenn Markoe (1985) *Phoenician Bronze and Silver Bowls from Cyprus and the Mediterranean* Berkeley: University of California Press.
Sabatino Moscati (ed) (1988) *The Phoenicians* Milan: Bompiani.
Glenn Markoe (2000) *Phoenicians* London: The British Museum Press.
Edward Lipinski (2004) *Itineraria Phoenicia* Leuven: Peeters.
Richard Miles (2010) *Carthage Must Be Destroyed* London: Penguin.
Mark Woolmer (2017) *A Short History on the Phoenicians* London: I.B. Tauris.
Josephine Quinn (2017) *In Search of the Phoenicians* Princeton: Princeton University Press.
Helene Sader (2019) *The History and Archaeology of Phoenicia* Atlanta: SBL Press.

www.ingramcontent.com/pod-product-compliance
Lightning Source LLC
Chambersburg PA
CBHW050818090426
42737CB00021B/3428